100375

A Critique of Sociological Reasoning

A Critique of
Sociological
Reasoning

An Essay in Philosophical Sociology

CHARLES W. SMITH

Basil Blackwell · Oxford

ISBN 0 631 19490 8 hardback

ISBN 0 631 10161 6 paperback

RS
157669
301.01 SMIT

Printed in Great Britain by
Billing and Sons Ltd.
London, Guildford and Worcester

To Rita

Contents

Introductory Preface

The thoughts and themes presented in this study evolved gradually over a period of nearly twenty years; I can trace the roots of most back to my undergraduate studies in philosophy, though they did not begin to take on their present form until I began to study sociology. I make this point because I feel the reader may better understand this study by being aware of its biographical character: i.e., it is a response to intellectual questions experienced and formulated within a broad intellectual context by a specific person, rather than a consensual response to a more narrowly defined professional concern.

The unifying concern of this book is, as its title indicates, sociological reasoning; more specifically, it attempts to explain the system of basic concepts and unifying assumptions upon which sociological reasoning rests. My objective is two-fold: one, to place sociological reasoning within the broader context of human reasoning *per se*, and two, to enhance our ability to explain and understand social behaviour by presenting a clear, concise and integrated exposition of what may be called the sociological perspective.

In actual fact, as I shall attempt to show, there are a number of distinct sociological perspectives, all of which share certain basic conceptual elements. Some of these common elements are unique to sociology; others are shared by the perspectives of other social sciences. Shared or not, it is these conceptual forms and their role in sociological reasoning which are the main concern of this book. Though I advocate a fairly novel, if not new, theoretical orientation, it is not my intention to present any new sociological theory or theories. Neither is it my intention to praise or damn specific theoretical positions, though in the course of my analysis value judgements will be made and specific types of investigations will be supported. Though I will necessarily deal with numerous sociological theories past and present, it is not my intention to present a review of such theories. My goal is rather to present a critique of sociological reasoning.

The book has been subtitled *An Essay in Philosophical Sociology* because it aptly conforms to Simmel's conception of such a study, namely, one that is concerned with '. . . the conditions, fundamental concepts, and presuppositions of concrete re-search . . . (and the) . . . completions, connections, questions, and concepts that have no place in experience and in immediately objective knowledge.'[1] As I shall attempt to show, however, such studies are even more important for the future of sociology than Simmel contemplated.

The ideas contained in this book have evolved over a period of years in response to the ideas of numerous philosophers and social theorists. It is consequently difficult for me to place this study in any single intellectual tradition. Kant's influence, as well as that of the American pragmatists, James, Dewey, Mead, Peirce and C. I. Lewis, is clear. If I had to place it in a contemporary social scientific context, I would lean toward two social theorists often categorized as structuralists, namely Jean Piaget and Claude Levi-Strauss, since they most clearly emphasize the categories of mind stressed in this study. In spirit, if not in specifics, my study also has much in common with the more recent works of Habermas, Richard Bernstein, Harré and Secord and Anthony Giddens.[2]

One additional question deserves some comment. For whom is this book intended? I have used earlier drafts in both graduate and undergraduate social theory courses with success; they have also been used in courses in the philosophy of the social sciences. I have no doubt that others could use the book in such courses. More generally, however, it is intended for those persons, be they philosophers or sociologists, who are interested in sociology not merely as an aggregate of facts and concepts, but as a way of ac-counting for human behaviour.

I have tried to address the important issues that must be faced by anyone concerned with the nature and future of sociological reasoning and of sociology itself. As with any book, what one is likely to get out of it will be determined in part by what one brings to it. In all cases, however, it is hoped that a deeper, richer understanding and appreciation of sociological reasoning will be obtained.

Numerous people, too many to list, have given me invaluable support during the years I have wrestled with this book. Seven people, however, deserve special mention, more for their general encouragement than for specific textual suggestions: Lewis Coser, Kurt Wolff, Carroll Bourgh, Patty Kendall, Peter Manicas, Paul Secord and my wife, Rita.

My thanks are due in addition to Bryan Wilson for his invaluable help and advice and to my publisher, Basil Blackwell, especially Polly Steele, for their editorial help, suggestions, and co-operation.

I
The Intentionality and Modality of Social Behaviour

A. INTRODUCTORY COMMENTS

This study seeks to analyse the basic concepts and unifying assumptions of sociological reasoning. It deals with numerous concepts embodied in a range of theoretical perspectives. Those which are of primary concern in this study, however, are not these concepts, but rather certain concepts which underlie these more familiar theoretical constructs: i.e., concepts which serve as the basic categories of sociological reasoning and experience. More specifically, it focuses upon (1) various notions of behaviour *per se*, (2) on what might be called the 'dimensions' of such behaviours, (3) on various analytical notions of 'unity' which govern the sociological conceptions of social groups, and (4) on the 'logics' and 'rationalities' of different types of meaning systems. These concerns are sufficiently different from those of most analyses of sociology to deserve some clarification.

That 'reality' is defined in terms of different perspectives is a generally accepted view; in sociology, it could even be considered a truism. This does not mean that all views of reality are equally useful. It is possible to claim that some perspectives are more 'objective' than others.[1] Such claims, of course, must be based upon some criteria, which in turn, are determined by different perspectives. Initially this process may appear to be circular, with different perspectives asserting their own validity in terms of their own criteria. In part this is true. Nevertheless, when such perspectives themselves are analysed, various principles and criteria not related to those perspectives often become operative: so that the process of analysis entails a pattern of thought whereby more universal criteria emerge.

Historically, two sorts of criteria have most often been offered as the final arbiters of reality: empirical criteria and rational criteria.[2] Unfortunately, neither kind has ever been proven to the satisfaction of all. The problem, simply put, is that neither experience—no matter how immediate—nor reason—no matter how abstract or pure—appears to be perspective-free. As a consequence, most have more recently followed the search for a different path in the search for objective knowledge. Attempts have been made not to transcend perspective, but to discover the essential character of perspective in general. The key historical figure in this philosophic revolution has been Immanuel Kant.[3]

Kant, writing in the late eighteenth century, attempted to lay the theoretical foundation for the possibility of scientific knowledge of the world as experienced. Despite the successes of seventeenth and eighteenth-century science, the fundamental claim of science as 'objective' knowledge had been questioned by David Hume's analysis, which revealed that 'empirical' knowledge was not 'necessary' knowledge.[4] Man, Hume argued, could not claim to perceive a necessary order in the external, empirical world. Kant answered that such necessity was due to conceptual elements that were intrinsic to reason itself and hence similar for all men. Kant was not pushing for a return to what is often called 'continental rationalism', where reality is defined as that which conforms to the dictates of pure reason.[5] Rather, he argued that all men of necessity structure the world of appearances, by which he meant the world as empirically experienced, in terms of various categories of experience. Consequently, 'objective', empirical knowledge was possible. In this way, Kant attempted to integrate the empirical and rational conceptions of reality and knowledge.

The basic elements specified by Kant were as follows: (1) The world as experienced is a spatial-temporal world; we experience the world in a spatial-temporal matrix. (2) We experience the world primarily as a world of objects. Here Kant argued that the notion of an object in general, what he called the 'concept of the object X', was a pure category of experience which man used to order his experiences. As Kant pointed out, we do not actually experience objects; we experience only various qualities and these we put together to form what we call 'objects' of our experiences. In other words, the concept of object with which we order these sensations is something which man imposes on these qualities. In its pure form 'the concept of the object X' is the notion of something in space and time within which various qualities are seen to inhere. (3) The dimensions, characteristics, traits or qualities of objects as experienced are those which correspond to our five senses. Objects can be experienced only in terms of those dimensions which we are capable of experiencing through our senses, e.g., colour, shape, smell, hardness, etc. In short, the world as empirically experienced is a world of objects in space and time exhibiting various sensory qualities.

Kant recognized that the world is not experienced as a static world. Objects act on other objects and things change. Furthermore, such changes often exhibit regularity. When such regularities are observed, man assumes a necessary connection between the various elements which constitute the event. This, Kant argued, was due to another category of experience, causality, which entails conceiving of one event, the cause, as necessarily bringing about another event, the effect. Such necessity, Kant argued, is not itself experienced; all that is experienced is regularity. The notion of necessity resided in man himself; more specifically, it was due to the notion of causality which itself was part of the conceptual apparatus through which man structured his experiences.

By positing these categories of experience,[6] Kant was able to admit the conceptual element of all empirical knowledge, yet to maintain that such knowledge was 'objective'. Since all knowledge of the 'external world' was structured in terms of these categories of experience, Kant put a barrier between man and the external world; what the world was like in and of itself, Kant's *Ding an sich*, could never be known. For Kant this barrier was fine, since it enabled him to leave room for religion. In short, Kant justified the claims of scientific knowledge by limiting its province.

Today, few scientists or philosophers of science accept Kant's position in its entirety. Most however, do accept his basic insight that empirical knowledge requires a conceptual frame of reference.[7] Similarly, many accept the object frame of reference as the right one for scientific knowledge, though most reject its necessary character. This is not surprising, since whatever its ontological or epistemological status, the object frame of reference has proved immensely useful for the physical sciences. It is similarly not surprising, given the success of the physical sciences, to find that many have attempted to use this frame of reference to order and to explain human behaviour.

Unfortunately, human behaviour often does not lend itself to the explanations used in the physical sciences. Human behaviour 'appears' to entail elements such as intentions, meanings, values and beliefs which are not 'real' in Kant's object frame of reference. They cannot be described in terms of sensory dimensions.

As a result, most social theorists have been forced to introduce and use frames of references which differ from Kant's. This, however, has raised questions regarding the objectivity of the knowledge generated by these other frames of reference. The problem basically is that objectivity requires that there be a basis for knowledge which is analytically independent of individual minds. If there is to be knowledge at all, however, this independent order must be, in principle, accessible to individual minds. Kant argued that his 'object frame of reference' satisfied both of these criteria because it was governed by what he called 'categories of experience'. For social theorists to claim that their knowledge has a degree of objectivity equal to that of the physical sciences, they must be able to make similar claims regarding their frames of reference.

The issue is further complicated by the fact that different social theorists make use of different frames of reference, which vary in the types of strains they put upon the object frame of reference. The key notion in all cases seems to be the concept of behaviour used. Apart from the physiological psychologist, who basically uses the physical science notion of behaviour, social scientists conceive of behaviour differently from the way in which it is conceived by physical scientists. How much their notions of behaviour differ from that of the physical scientists, however, vary. All incorporate what I would call 'ideational' elements, i.e., intentions, meanings, values and beliefs. Some perspectives, however, incorporate more than do others. [8]

This essay is primarily concerned with the sociological perspective and hence with its modifications. These modifications are, however, very radical because sociology, of all the social sciences, incorporates within its perspective the widest range of ideational elements. It is useful, therefore, to begin by analysing the simpler modifications required by other social sciences.[9]

To understand the basic problem that confronts social scientists, one need only ponder the differences between a rock free of all movement and a person free of all movement. A rock at rest requires little or no explanation; explanation is required only to explain its movement. Rocks do not move by themselves. Persons and animals do. On the other hand, a person or animal free of motion, i.e., holding a frozen position, normally requires explanation. The reason for this is that we normally use different frames of reference when dealing with animal behaviour and physical behaviour. We experience the physical world as a passive world, whereas we experience the world of living creatures as an active world.

In the world of physical objects, actions are conceived as reactions to forces of varying types. To describe and analyse such actions, we need only be able to receive the proper information regarding these forces. This is exactly what Kant claimed his categories of experience do; they define what is 'empirically real' and hence what can function as real forces in this world of objects. In the social world of man, actions are perceived as the results not only of external forces but also of the intentions of actors. The qualities which are important in describing and analysing such actions consequently are not simply or even mainly the qualities which may appear to pertain to objects, but rather the qualities which appear to be significant to the various actors.

There are both similarities and differences between the categories of passive experience which constitute Kant's object frame of reference and the categories of active experience which constitute what could be called the intentional frame of reference.[10] Both frames of reference make use of spatial and temporal dimensions and both use the notion of the object X as a unifying category. Both also entail a subject-object relational view of knowledge. In the intentional frame of reference, however, the notion of the object X does not refer primarily to the notion of a thing in space and time; rather it refers primarily to things which can object, resist, stand off from man, i.e. objects exist only insofar as they exist for someone. This distinction is analogous to the active-passive distinction noted above. In the object frame of reference the primary meaning of object is 'being in space and time'. In the intentional frame of reference the primary meaning of object is that which is in relationship to someone, i.e. that which is the focus of someone's concern.

To restate the issue in a slightly different way, in the object frame of reference, objects are accepted because they exist in space and time; because they exist and we exist in space and time and because of the laws of space and time, they can resist us. In the intentional frame of reference, objects exist insofar as they are in relationship to us and exist for us; the positing of their independent existence is a secondary act of materialization.

There are analogous differences in the meanings attributed to space and time by the two frames of reference. In the object frame of reference space and time are seen as neutral axes of a spatial-temporal matrix within which all that constitutes the world of appearances exist. In the intentional frame of reference, space and time are relative properties which specify the spatial and temporal distances between subject and object.

It is when one begins to analyse the dimensions which are central in characterizing objects in these two different frames of reference that the most important differences emerge. In the object frame of reference, the key dimensions are sensory; in the intentional frame of reference, the key dimensions are intentional. That is, the qualities used to define objects in the intentional frame of reference are determined by, and hence analogous to, man's basic concerns towards the objects. Pain and pleasure reflect such a concern and constitute such a dimension. To understand why man should define his world in these terms, let us examine man as an intentional being. To do this, it is useful to look at man as he comes into the world as a newborn infant.[11]

The newborn infant has one objective—to survive. Maybe this remains the basic objective of all human beings throughout their lives, but survival takes a simpler form in newborn infants than it does in mature adults. To the infant, survival depends simply on getting what he needs and eliminating what is not needed. It is in terms of these processes that pleasure and pain emerge. When the infant gets what he wants and eliminates what he does not want, he experiences pleasure; when he does not get what he wants and when he cannot eliminate what he does not want, he experiences pain. His wants, in turn, are determined by biological needs.

At birth a human infant's needs are much like those of any newborn animal. He needs nourishment, warmth and the ability to excrete. He also needs love; he must be the object upon whom others of his species focus attention and care. Even in the case of love, the input-output model described above holds. A newborn infant truly consumes the psychic energy concentrated upon him.

As a child matures his needs change. He continues to rely heavily, however, on the gratification dimension in defining his world. Furthermore, this dimension continues to be used to divide the world into those things which satisfy needs and those things which thwart needs. In social contexts these needs, and hence the gratification dimension, most often apply to libidinal inputs and outputs.

While gratification may be ontogenetically the primary intentional dimension, it is not the only one. There is also the power dimension. This dimension categorizes objects and people in terms of the degree to which they are subject to one's will. [12] Here again it is useful to look at the human infant.

As noted above, newborn infants rely almost exclusively upon the gratification dimension in defining the world about them. This is due to the fact that at birth an infant does not really have a will. He has wants but he does not experience these wants as 'his' wants, because initially the child does not separate himself from the rest of his world; it is all a single confused mass. Within a few months, however, the child begins to distinguish his sense of self from his experiences of other things. He also becomes aware of the fact that he can make certain, but not other, things happen by an act of will. He can make his hand move, but not the door; he can control his own crying, but not the coming and going of his mother. In short, some experiences are experienced as flowing from his own will whereas others are experienced as happening to him.

The extent to which things and people conform or object to his will becomes very important to the child. At one level it is important because the child learns to recognize the relationship between the power he possesses in a given situation (that which he can control by an act of will) and his ability to obtain certain types of gratification. Being cuddled by his mother may be pleasurable, but such attention can be obtained only by mother's cooperation; the extent to which she can be controlled, therefore, has direct implications upon his pleasure. In addition, the child seems to seek power *per se*.

Perhaps his desire for power simply reflects the fact that power is one of his basic needs, like love. Given the fact that all individuals must possess some degree of power to survive, such a position is reasonable. Analytically, however, power differs from these other needs in that it is not something consumed by the infant. Power is concerned rather with spheres of influence. The positive feelings associated with having power are, in short, different from the pleasures associated with satisfying organic needs. Whereas gratification values are determined by the way things satisfy or thwart our input-output needs, power values are determined by the extent to which things are controlled by and/or control our wills. Analytically, therefore, they deserve to be treated independently. [13]

People obviously use other intentional dimensions in defining their world. But as these dimensions do not function at the 'raw', non-cognitive level with which we have so far been dealing, [14] I shall not introduce them here.

Though the intentional frame of reference differs from the object frame of reference, it still presents us with an external world. Admittedly, it is more difficult to describe this world objectively since its relevant characteristics depend more on how people respond to the world, (or how we interpret these responses) than do those of the world of the physical sciences. In principle, however, there is nothing non-objective about an intentionally construed world. It may be more difficult to achieve a professional consensus regarding proper procedures, etc. Despite all this, one can still claim that his research conforms to the canons of empirical science insofar as it reflects regularities which pertain to an objectively given 'real' world, i.e. a world which must conform to empirical observations.

A person so inclined could, in fact, claim that the physical sciences make use of a modified form of the intentional frame of reference. The writings of Whitehead and Bergson provide an ontological basis for arguing for the intentional character of all being, and the writings of a number of American pragmatists such as C. I. Lewis and John Dewey provide a basis for making an analogous argument on epistemological grounds. [15] It is not my purpose, however, to argue the intentional character of the object frame of reference. [16] My purpose has rather been to introduce the intentional frame of reference, emphasizing its 'scientific' character.

In its simplest form, i.e. when restricted to raw or non-cognitive behaviour, the intentional frame of reference lends itself admirably to the behaviourist/neo-behaviourist view of human behaviour. Many behaviourists, of course, would claim that they have no need for the intentional frame of reference. They prefer to believe that the object frame of reference of the physical sciences is adequate for their needs. In support of their position, they argue that they, like the physical scientists, are only interested in behaviour. I would argue that this is not the case. Behaviour for the behaviourist is not the same as behaviour for the physical scientist. To the physical scientist, behaviour means physical change, i.e. the movement of physical matter in space and time. To the behaviourist, it is a response to some stimulus which in one form or other is conceived as 'experienced' by the actor in question. [17]

This issue, however, is not, for the purposes at hand, of major concern, since whether or not specific behaviourists admit to using the intentional rather than an object frame of reference, the fact remains that for most people, human behaviour lends itself better to the intentional frame of reference than it does to the object frame of reference. What constitutes a much more serious problem is the fact that raw, non-cognitive behaviour, even when approached in terms of the intentional frame of reference, is a notion that covers only a limited amount of human behaviour. A few simple examples may help to clarify this issue.

A three-month-old baby is offered a bottle of milk. The baby grasps the bottle in his mouth and then rejects it. It is offered again, grasped and again rejected. The mother checks the temperature and finds it pleasantly warm. She then puts the nipple to her own mouth and discovers that it has a very bitter soapy taste.

Al and Betty, a young married couple, sit down to their regular Thursday night dinner of meatballs and spaghetti. After a few mouthfuls, Al comments that the meatballs taste different. He is not sure whether he likes the new taste or not, but it is unusual. Betty agrees but cannot understand why since she claims to have used her regular recipe. As she is talking she glances over at the stove and lets out a loud gasp. Al looks over at the stove and lets out a similar gasp. Both have observed that on the stove sits their insect poison in a container very similar to their salt shaker. Both reach the same conclusion: the strange taste is due to the fact that Betty has inadvertently used insect poison rather than salt in making the meatballs. They both rush to the bathroom and induce vomiting.

Jane and Bill have been invited to dinner by a friend whom most would consider a 'food freak'. He is concerned about the world running out of food and as a consequence is continually experimenting with new recipes which rely on untapped resources. This evening he is serving a curried meat dish of some sort. Jane and Bill find it quite delicious, but are uncertain what it is. After finishing their dinners, they finally get their friend to tell them what it was that they ate. He tells them curried rat. They both become violently nauseated and just make it to the bathroom in time.

Each of these episodes deals with human behaviour. Furthermore, each is readily understandable from a common sense perspective; it seems clear why the baby rejected the bottle, why Al and Betty rushed to the bathroom and induced vomiting, and why Jane and Bill became violently nauseated. What is perhaps not as obvious is that each of these episodes utilizes a different notion of human behaviour. The episode of the baby utilizes what could be called level I behaviour, i.e. simple stimulus-response behaviour. The meatball and spaghetti episode, in contrast, utilizes what could be called level II behaviour, i.e. meaningful behaviour, while the curried rat episode makes use of what could be called level III behaviour, i.e. normative behaviour. The baby acts in response to an unpleasant stimulus. Al and Betty act in response to an interpreted, meaningful reality. Jane and Bill act in response to a set of governing expectations. The key point is that our understanding of each of these episodes makes use of a different conception of behaviour.

Of these three episodes only the first, the baby rejecting the bottle, utilizes a conception of behaviour which conforms to the criteria of the intentional frame of reference as so far developed. The other episodes rely on elements—meanings and expectations—which have so far not been justified. To do this, such meanings and expectations must be shown to have some sort of 'objective' status.[18]

For the purposes of justifying meaning as objectively 'real', the works of George Herbert Mead are of special importance.[19] Mead was concerned with the question, 'How is society possible?' More specifically, he was concerned with the analytic relationship between man as a biological organism and man as a being capable of reasoning and meaningful communication. What is unique about Mead's analysis is that human meanings and reasonings are: (1) treated as ideational processes, i.e. they are not reduced to brain processes, and (2) analysed within a behaviouristic frame of reference, i.e. they are explained in terms of observable human behaviour rather than in terms of unobservable subjective processes.

Mead began his analysis by observing that man is biologically a social creature. Men are born into social units and spend most of their lives with others of their species. In this regard, man is not unique. Numerous other species, e.g., sheep, wolves, bees, ants, and monkeys, exhibit such social tendencies. Given that all other 'social' animals can be observed to engage in what Mead calls 'exchange of gestures', it is not surprising that men also should have developed this capacity. Such exchanges, however, do not constitute what we would call meaningful communication; rather they entail what Mead calls the exchange of signs gestures. A simple sign as defined by Mead is something which calls forth a specific behavioural response; it has no recognized meaning.[20]

Many species engage in such exchanges. Animal A does x and animal B responds by doing y; animal A then responds to y by doing z, etc. Animals engage in such exchanges in many different situations: mating, protection of territory, foraging for food, etc. In none of these situations do we have to assume that the animals in question have any understanding of what they are doing. With human beings, however, we assume some sort of understanding. Mead felt that before we could treat such understanding as a scientifically verifiable fact, it was necessary to explain how it evolved.

Mead's explanation is based on two main points: first, man's greater brain capacity, and secondly, and most importantly, man's reliance upon verbal gestures. Man's reliance on verbal gestures in combination with his inherent, organic, neurological abilities is what makes meaningful communication possible. These factors make meaningful communication possible for the following reasons: (1) Verbal gestures differ from other gestures, e.g., facial expressions, body movement, etc., in that they are received by the sender as well as by the intended receiver. We do not see our own frowns but we do hear our own sounds. (2) As a result of the fact that we receive our own signs, we call out in ourselves the responses associated with the sign. Normally, the sender's response to his own sign is drowned out by the response of the intended receiver. When for some reason or other the intended receiver does not respond, the sender is likely to experience his own response clearly.

When we give an instruction like 'close the door', for example, we hear what we say but do not actively respond to our own command. If the person to whom the command is directed fails to act, however, it is not unusual to find ourselves responding to our own command; we find ourselves almost inadvertently moving to close the door. When this happens, i.e., when we call out in ourselves the proper response to the given sign, we forge a link between the sign and its response within ourselves. A link of sorts already existed. Without it we would not be able to respond properly to any signs nor could we expect others to respond properly. Previous to the events depicted above, however, this link is not grasped within a single being. The sign is given by one person and the response is experienced by another person. When a sign and its response are linked in a single joint experience, the sign comes to have a meaning, for the meaning of a thing is simply the responses which it can call forth. (Since the sign/act previously had a designated response, we can say that it always had its own meaning, but this meaning was not attached to the sign.)

While this definition of 'meaning' may appear far-fetched, it proves eminently sound when applied to concrete objects. What do we mean by 'tree'? The image of a tree comes to mind, but the image is not its meaning. Well, a tree is something to climb; it is made of wood from which we can make many other things; birds live in trees; trees can provide shade, etc. Similarly, what is meant by 'dog'? It is an animal which likes people; it also has sharp teeth, a good sense of smell, and good hearing. All of these meanings have something in common. They point to a potential response which the thing may stimulate. A tree may be something that we might climb, something which we might cut down, something in which we might look for birds, or something we would use for shade. A dog might be something to play with, something to avoid, or something to use as a sentry.

It is in the analyses of human reasoning that the true power of Mead's conception of meaning as expected responses becomes apparent. It is man's ability to reason that is generally seen to be the crucial factor that separates him from all other species; reasoning, however, can only occur in terms of meanings. This becomes obvious when we analyse the reasoning process itself.

What does man do when he reasons? Starting with a given situation, he considers the various situations which might follow. Each of these situations is then analysed in terms of the various chain of events which might result from it. This is possible only if one can conceptualize what may be expected to follow each specific situation which makes up the chain. This we do by considering the meaning of each situation; we ask ourselves if we do x, what will this mean, i.e. what will follow? In short, reasoning entails that we think through the various sign-response possibilities. This we are able to do because, in Mead's terminology, we are able to think in terms of symbols by which he means 'meaningful signs', i.e. signs with attached responses. [21]

In analysing how meanings come into being, Mead makes two points which bear on our earlier discussion: (1) His analysis implicitly, if not explicitly, underscores the basic intentionality of human behaviour; he assumes that man's world is defined in terms of man's interests towards it. (2) His analysis reveals that man's world is multi-level; there is the world of non-reflective experience—Mead's world of signs—and the world of meanings/symbols. In the terminology of this study, level I and level II behaviour.

Mead makes other points as well; he considered that the most important of these is that meanings are social, because for a meaning to arise there must be both agreed-upon sets and actual exchanges of gestures. A man cannot generate a meaning on his own. Consequently, man as a thinking being is social in nature. [22]

In placing man in a meaningful world and in making meanings social, Mead adds a new and important dimension to the strict behaviourist's conception of human behaviour. Whereas we have seen that physical action can be seen as a response to forces describable in terms of sensory dimensions, human behaviour is seen as a response to stimuli defined in terms of intentional dimensions. If, as Mead asserts, the stimuli to which men respond are normally meaningful, and if such meanings are social in nature, then the stimuli of human behaviour must be defined in terms of intentional dimensions *whose specific values are themselves socially determined.* In short, man's world must be seen as reflecting a social process, as well as a psychological process. [23]

Although Mead starts from a behaviouristic position, he ends up by modifying it dramatically. He does this not by rejecting elements within the behaviourist's perspective, but by adding new elements, the most significant of which are meanings. By incorporating meanings into the behaviourist's perspective Mead does more than simply add something new; he, in effect, redefines the basic parameters of the perspective. More specifically, he redefines the properties/dimensions of objects and their relationships.

To say that Mead, in effect, redefines the basic properties/dimensions of objects may initially appear to be an overstatement. [24] The gratification and power dimensions used by behaviourists would still seem to be the primary dimensions even in a meaningful world. To conceive of objects, be they persons or things, as pleasurable or powerful in the sense that these are the meanings attributed to the objects, however, is quite different from simply experiencing (in a non-cognitive manner) them as pleasurable or powerful. Admittedly, meanings are, according to Mead, based upon such non-cognitive experiences but they are nevertheless qualitatively different. The key to this difference is the temporal and social character of meanings as compared to raw or non-cognitive experiences.

More specifically, the here and now of a meaningful world, in contrast to the here and now of a world devoid of meanings, is, to use Mead's term, 'undifferentiated'. The *here* reaches out to distant places while the *now* reaches out to both the past and the future. This is what meanings do; they relate what is here and now to things which are not here and now. To describe a meaningful world, or any segment of it, as it is here and now, consequently requires a similar reaching out to things which in a strictly physical sense are not in the here and now. To define a thing as pleasurable or powerful (i.e. to assign such meanings), implies, for example, not merely that the thing serves as the stimuli for a pleasurable or power experience, but that it normally generates such experiences. It is the expectation of such experiences which is the essence of meanings.

This qualitative difference between a meaningful world and a world devoid of meanings leads to other differences: (1) It calls for the notion of empirical observation to be modified; (2) It allows for the introduction of a new intentional dimension; and (3) It introduces 'new' notions of causal relationships.

The required modification of our notion of empirical observation follows directly from the points just made regarding the here and now of a meaningful world. It is obviously more difficult to describe such a world objectively. Where is one to draw one's lines? One may rely on the statements of one's subjects as to the meaning of their acts; subjects, unfortunately, are often unaware of the 'true' meanings of their acts, i.e. what will follow. Or one can attempt to draw one's lines in terms of the activities which appear to be relevant to the act under investigation;[25] here, one faces the possibility, however, of simply missing what is actually the meaning of the act to those engaged in it. In most situations, consequently, a mixed approach is necessary, but this often makes it more difficult to achieve a professional consensus as to what is going on.

To say that something is difficult to achieve does not mean that it is impossible. One can still claim to be dealing with an 'objective' world. It is not the 'real' world of the strict behaviourist (to say nothing of the physical scientist) in so far as it entails not only intentional dimensions but meanings. These meanings, however, are not 'subjective', i.e. subject to the whims of individual minds. They are rather products of man's biological and social nature. As such they are part of an objective world and can in principle be known 'objectively'. One can, in fact, make a good case that in the light of Mead's analysis of meaning, all knowledge insofar as knowledge entails meaning is objective only in this social sense.[26]

The new dimension introduced by meanings is utility, or, as it is often conceived, 'economic/labour value'.[27] This dimension is directly related to the notion of expectations discussed above. Once meanings and expectations are introduced, it becomes possible to classify things in terms of their future uses in general. To talk of a thing as having potential uses entails seeing the thing as having within it 'labour equivalencies'. The crux of this new awareness is the recognition that other entities respond and act not only in accordance to wills but in accordance with their physical surroundings, much of which can be affected by what may be called work. Put in a developmental context, the child learns that he can affect his world not only by willing this or that but by acting in specific ways. He learns that he can even affect the behaviour of other people in this way, since he can often get others to do on their own what he desires because of changes he brings about by his own labour.

The one- to two-year old child discovers, for example, that while his parents are becoming more and more immune to his crying (a straight power technique when used to get parents to do what is wanted), they (his parents) get very excited and pleased when he manages to put those different shaped objects into those different shaped holes. He further learns that not only can he get people to respond to such activities but that he is able to obtain certain results which he was not able to directly by means of his will. He learns that while he cannot will his mobile to move, he can make it move by striking it with his hand.

This insight—that the world can be manipulated through labour—brings with it a whole new way of looking at the world. It is now seen not only in terms of gratification and power dimensions, but in terms of the labour required to maintain it or change it; defined in this way, labour value is intentional because, like gratification and power, it defines the world in terms of the way the world responds to our needs and intentions. Generally, the types of activities which qualify as labour are activities which entail the use of hands.[28]

Of all the modifications of the scientific perspective necessitated by including meanings, perhaps the most fundamental is that which bears on the concept of causality. As noted earlier, the scientist, whatever his concern, is interested in doing more than objectively describing the world. He is also interested in accounting for change. To a scientist this requires discovering the underlying regularities and order of such change. For the physical scientist and the strict behaviourist, such regularities and order are usually conceived in terms of what is called 'efficient causality', i.e. the cause is seen as preceding the effect in time and as bringing about the effect.

For the physical scientist and the strict behaviourist only efficient causality makes any sense because only this conforms to their conception of the temporal character of the 'real world'. The world exists in the here and now; a here and now which reflects its past but not its future. The world as a meaningful entity, however, is affected by expectations of the future. This not only allows but requires introducing other notions of causality; more specifically, it requires introducing what MacIver refers to as a teleological nexus, i.e. causes which are seen to follow the effect in time.[29] Such a teleological nexus, however, does not negate the traditional scientific conception of order as repeatable chain of events. To explain a thing still means to place it within an ordered chain of events; the chain of events may run into the future as well as into the past, but the basis for the explanation is similar. It does, however, greatly expand the very limited concept of causal relationship which has reigned supreme in the physical sciences until quite recently.[30]

To return to our example of Al and Betty. To understand their behaviour. it is necessary to see them as acting within a meaningful context. They did not run to the bathroom because they saw a particular object, but because of what that object meant to them. Their act of inducing vomiting similarly cannot be explained in terms of their response to the meatballs and spaghetti, but rather to their understanding of what was contained in the meatballs.

B. SOCIOLOGY AND NORMATIVE BEHAVIOUR

In the preceding pages some of the modifications of the 'scientific' perspective, as formulated by Kant, necessitated by the inclusion of various elements characteristic of human behaviour have been reviewed. What may well be, from a theoretical point of view, the most troubling aspect of human behaviour, namely, its 'normative' properties, however, have not yet been discussed. These normative properties are of special importance for this study because they, more than any other aspect of human behaviour, are most directly related to the sociological perspective. To understand the 'what, how and why' of these normative properties, it is useful to return to Mead.

Mead, despite his emphasis upon the social bases of meanings, was a social psychologist not a sociologist. Consequently, he never pushed his analysis to its 'sociological' conclusion, namely to the 'governing potential' of meanings. He did distinguish between 'significant others', (specific individuals to whom we relate), and 'generalized others', (unified/organized groups to whom we relate); he did this quite clearly in his analysis of play and games.[31] For Mead, however, the expectations of the generalized other are the unified, organized and, consequently, more abstract expectations of the individual significant others making up the generalized other. In many situations, however, the meanings, beliefs and expectations of groups are more than the sum of the meanings, beliefs and values of their individual members; they are unique to the group itself.[32] This is one, if not the key, sociological insight into the nature of human behaviour. How and why this should occur is another question, and to answer it, it is necessary to determine why man bothers with meanings in the first place.

Though Mead does not deal with this question directly (he treats the emergence of meanings as part of the natural evolutionary process), the underlying reason is clearly to aid man by making his world a more ordered place.[33] If this is so, then it makes sense that man, where possible, would attempt to organize his meanings into ordered meaning systems. For this a high degree of consensus is necessary, which is possible only when the individuals are themselves organized in some way, when they constitute some sort of group.

All meanings require consensus. The objectives of such a consensus, however, can and do vary. In the case of a simple set of interacting individuals, the objective is normally limited to avoiding and circumventing disagreement; when the individuals involved constitute a group of some sort, the objective may be to generate an ordered account. In other words, the more organized the individuals, generally the more organized the meanings, beliefs and values of the group so that the meanings, beliefs and values of the group will constitute a unified, organized meaning/belief/value system. The rules governing behaviour in an open marketplace such as a flea market or local bazaar, for example, are not as formally integrated as those governing behaviour within a bureaucratic organization.

The line dividing unorganized networks from organized groups is often fuzzy; networks merge into groups and vice versa. The fact that organized groups act to generate a meanings system, whereas unorganized networks simply generate meanings rests upon the degree of consensus which each is capable of generating. The more organized the group, the greater the potential consensus, the more likely a meanings system.

Meaning systems, in and of themselves, do not in principle add anything new to human behaviour. They simply reflect the fact that the meanings that man imposes on the world are themselves interrelated. In substance, Mead makes this point himself. In point of fact they do add something new, namely, what is generally called the 'normative' property of meanings. To understand this normative property it is necessary to recognize that meanings are not necessarily passive. They do more than reflect experiences; meanings in the form of expectations can and do determine how men respond and act. [34] An example might help to clarify this.

To survive man must eat. In the process of consuming various foods man has various experiences. Some foods are more pleasurable than others. As a result of these experiences and the experiences of others, man comes to have certain expectations regarding different foods. These expectations are built into the meanings attributed to the foods in question. These meanings, once attributed, however, may become integrated into an encompassing meaning system. Once this occurs, the meaning system itself can and usually does put limits on the meaning. The meaning is no longer based solely on the experiences; the meaning system imposes its own restraints.

Admittedly, the other meanings making up the meaning system are themselves based upon experiences. The range of experiences relevant to the meaning system, however, is much broader than the experiences related to the specific meaning in question. The possibility of conflicting experiences, which would favour conflicting categorizations, consequently arises. If the meaning system as a whole is to be maintained, it is necessary that certain experiences be rejected. To return to Jane and Bill.

We could assume that if they had been told before they ate the dish that it was curried rat they would not have enjoyed it. In fact it is highly doubtful that they would even have tasted it. Here then we find meanings governing experiences and behaviour. The meaning does not merely indicate an expected experience; it is part of an overall ordered account of reality. The meaning is determined by the system of meanings to which it belongs.

Meaning systems differ in the amount of behavioural conformity that they require and are capable of producing. Generally, the more inclusive and integrated the meaning system, the more normative it is likely to be. People who are convinced they know what is, are likely to be more convinced that they also know what should be done than are those who are not so sure that they know what is. Similarly, the more integrated and established the group, the more likely that its meaning system will be integrated; the more tightly organized a group, the more likely there will be a tight party line. Consequently, when one is dealing with established groups one is most likely to discover normatively governed behaviour.

Such groups are the special interest of the sociologist; not surprisingly, therefore, we find that it is the sociologist who most relies on normative explanations of human behaviour.

Meaning/normative systems entail their own modifications of our conception of human behaviour. These modifications, while different in substance from those required by the notions of human experience and meanings *per se*, are similar in form. More specifically, they deal with: (1) the dimensions of the social world; (2) the problem of 'objective' observation; and (3) the canons of theoretical order.

For the most part, meaning systems deal with those meanings already discussed, namely, gratification, power and utility/economic meanings. Meaning systems by their very nature, however, introduce a new dimension which I shall refer to as an 'ordering' dimension.[35] This ordering dimension is without doubt the most complex of what have now become four intentional dimensions; it is also from a sociological point of view the most important. Its importance and complexity is due to the fact that it often subsumes the other three dimensions. To understand how this can occur, as well as to understand the basic properties of this dimension, it is useful to re-examine some of the points covered in our analysis of meaning/normative systems.

In examining the emergence of meaning systems, man's concern for an ordered view of the world was stressed. The very act of categorizing experiences, especially at the level of meanings, reflects a concern with order. The specific dimension used may be of intrinsic importance to man, but it is only insofar as they allow man to divide and lump things together in terms of what he can expect from them, that they are of any practical use. It is only at the *meaning system* level of human experience, however, that this concern for order becomes explicit, and it then generates what I have called an ordering dimension. So it is only at the meaning system level of human experience, that man becomes concerned with the ordering quality of things: a quality that does not reflect the internal order of the thing itself, but rather the thing's ability to bring order to our view of the world, i.e. to strengthen our meaning systems.

That objects, be they persons or things, may contribute order or disorder to our accounts of reality may initially seem implausible; closer scrutiny, however, reveals that it is not only plausible but quite normal. Religious leaders and intellectuals have traditionally been held in high esteem because they were able to show the underlying order of events which to others appeared unordered. They were able to provide acceptable accounts. Parents often do the same with their children. In contrast, other individuals are often the source of disorder; they continually give disparate interpretations to events. The 'mentally ill' are a good example of this latter type. In fact, our very notions of esteem and prestige are used by and large to classify people in terms of the degree of order they offer.[36]

Things also can serve as the source of order and disorder.[37] The Bible and other books of law function in this way. Various symbolic objects function in a similar way. The flag of the United States of America, in symbolically representing the original thirteen colonies with the additional states, says something about the basic structure of the country. The cross is an ordering object to most Christians. It serves as a symbol by which the physical world and God's world are integrated. This integration is based on the fact that the cross represents the crucifixion which revealed Jesus to be both man (he died and suffered) and God (he was reborn and immortal). Such objects are generally referred to as sacred or holy. (It is interesting to note that the term 'holy' itself insofar as it is derived from the word 'whole' implies integration.) In contrast, other objects such as human faeces are a source of disorder, because they stimulate conflicting responses. Faeces are of us and as such deserve to be treated as we treat ourselves; they are also not us and as such should be treated as something different.

The basic disorderly aspect of faeces and the strains they create become apparent when one observes the difficulty children have in learning how to respond to their own faeces. Initially, if allowed, they treat them as they would their hands or toes. They are theirs and stimulate basically the same responses that they have towards the rest of their own bodies. They play with them, smell them, etc. They are told that they are not theirs, that they are foreign and dirty. Often when so instructed children will begin to treat other parts of their bodies as foreign and dirty. (It might be noted that the notion of dirt itself entails a sense of disorder as when it is used to imply untidy or things out of place.) Children can be observed attempting to push away their feet with such comments as 'dirty', 'don't touch', etc. They soon learn that it is only their faeces which are dirty, not their feet, etc., but the underlying contradictory nature of the so-called proper responses remains. It remains with most of us throughout our lives. We are generally not aware of any such contradictory response because such stimuli are normally endowed with what is called a taboo quality; they are rejected as bad but with the additional provision that we are simply to accept their badness, not hope to explain it. Most of us, for example, are much more put off by a jar of urine than we are by a jar of acid, though the acid is potentially much more dangerous than the urine.

One can test this by asking friends whether they would be more put off by finding human body hairs in the bath at a hotel or mud from some shoe. Most will say that they would be more put off by the body hairs though such hairs were no doubt well washed while the mud from the workman's shoe could contain a wide range of caustic and/or infectious elements. Most of us are similarly much more put off by the idea of mother-son incest than we are by simple adultery. The reason is that incest taboos entail basic contradictions. On the one hand we are told to love, in fact to love physically, our parents but not to engage in or even fantasize about actual love-making with them. Adultery in contrast is simply something that we are told not to do.

It is now possible to see why the ordering dimension can be said to subsume the other intentional dimensions. While the ordering dimension is concerned with order *per se*, that which is ordered is usually described in terms of the other dimensions. Consequently, to have an ordered view specific gratification, power, or economic values must be assigned to the world insofar as only specific values allow for an ordered view of the world.

The introduction of meaning/normative systems, not surprisingly, further complicates the task of obtaining 'objective' empirical data. The difficulty is two-fold: (1) there is a need to refocus one's attention upon social groupings[38] rather than on specific individuals; (2) there is a greater need to emphasize subjects' view of their world. The need to refocus upon social grouping is due to the fact that meaning systems belong to groups not individuals. Admittedly, such meaning systems are reflected in individual behaviour; if they weren't they wouldn't be of much interest. Individuals, however, are usually members of a number of different groups. To avoid becoming utterly confused, therefore, it is necessary to distinguish these groups from each other. Unfortunately, groups are usually more ambiguously defined than are individuals.

One's ability to find the relevant group is directly related to one's chances of grasping the relevant meaning system. Apart from just finding the relevant group, there is the problem of spelling out its meaning system. It is not enough to check subjects' statements against their behaviour, a technique which works quite well when dealing with meanings *per se*. This is because meanings in meaning systems are defined to a large extent in terms of other meanings within the meaning system. This forces one to rely even more heavily upon subjects' statements as to the meanings they hold. One is not forced to accept subjects' accounts at face value; one must still examine their behaviour. The task is complicated by the fact that it is not enough to look for 'obvious' relationships among such behaviour. Such obvious relationships are not sufficient because different meaning systems allow for and utilize a wide range of relationships and orders, which are not necessarily the sequential orders characteristic of the physical sciences.

To give an example. Someone may say that he doesn't eat mushrooms because they make him sick. When we secretly slip some mushrooms into his food, however, nothing happens. On the other hand, if he knowingly eats mushrooms, he does get sick. Question: do mushrooms make him sick? One might answer that mushrooms *per se* do not make him sick, but just the idea of mushrooms does. For most social scientists, however, such ideas are real; they are concerned with both the idea and the chemical compound. The problem, in short, is a real one.

To put the matter somewhat differently, behaviour may be seen to make sense if it can be related in some orderly way with something else. This can happen in a number of different ways depending upon what is the governing meaning system. Things can be ordered in terms of sets, i.e. each thing is placed in its proper category; things can be ordered in terms of the principles of greater than and less than; and/or things can be ordered in terms of 'if, then' relationships. Things can also be ordered in terms of various types of analogous forms. We will have an opportunity to return to this very important but complex issue later; for now, however, it is sufficient to restate the main point: meaning systems allow for different types of rationalities.

It should be stressed that reliance upon different senses of order does not make sociology unscientific. The sociologist is not free to use whatever order he chooses. *He must use the type of order that objective observations lead him to believe is operative in the situation under investigation. To use an order which objective observation does not indicate is so operative, even if this order has been enshrined as the 'order' of 'scientific reasoning', is in contrast highly unscientific.* [39]

While it is true that the task of determining the type of order of any meaning system, like the tasks of describing the content of a meaning system and the group to which the meaning system belongs, is dependent upon empirical observation, there are also certain underlying *a priori* elements. These are, to a large extent, inherent in the concept of order which applies to the given situation. [40] More specifically, the various notions of order which characterize social groupings and their respective meaning systems have their own *a priori* properties, which determine in great measure the nature of such groups and their meaning systems, as well as the theoretical accounts which are possible. My objective in Part II will be to examine these *a priori* properties. More specifically, I will examine the notions of 'unity' which underlie social groupings and their respective meaning systems.

That different notions of unity underlie different types of social groups is due to the fact that the patterns of social contact which give rise to such groupings themselves reflect different notions of unity. Men rely on different notions of unity in generating patterns of social contact; these notions of unity are themselves *a priori* categories of experience. Furthermore they affect the character of both the group and its meaning system; the character of these groups and meaning systems, in turn, determine the types of theoretical accounts which emerge. Put more colloquially, in forming social groups, different criteria for grouping are used; what is more, these different criteria affect the character of both the groups so formed and their associated meaning systems, to say nothing of the types of theoretical explanations which may be given.

Unfortunately but not surprisingly, from an analytical point of view the notion(s) of unity used in any given situation is (are) not always clearly defined. 'Real' social groups are commonly analytical hybrids; this complicates the task of analysis. I have elected, therefore, to focus my analysis upon various 'ideal types'.[41] This means that at times I shall have to deviate from the 'common view' regarding the nature of such social groups. I will do my best to relate my analysis to this common view, but the reader should remember that we shall be dealing with various ideal types.

C. REVIEW OF MAJOR POINTS OF PART I

This critique has so far been concerned with making the following points:

(1) Any social science, if it accepts 'human experiences' as 'real'—with the exception of physiological psychology this appears to include all the social sciences—is committed to an intentional frame of reference. The essential feature of this frame of reference is that objects are conceived not simply as entities in space and time but rather as entities which exist for man; the basic dimensions of

this frame of reference are a gratification and power dimension.

(2) Any social science which accepts meanings as 'real', which would include nearly all but the most extreme stimulus-response behaviourists, is further committed to a multi-level social world: a world characterized both by a 'utility/economic' dimension and to which multiple concepts of causality can be applied.

(3) The decision to accept meaning/normative systems as 'real', a policy which pertains primarily to sociology/anthropology, commits one to an even more complex view of the social world. It is a world that can be described in terms of an 'ordering' dimension, as well as the other three dimensions; a world in which meanings can govern behaviours; a world in which the basic units of analysis are social groups rather than individuals; a world whose basic order may reflect varying 'logical' forms.

Whereas man's ability to experience his environment is a biological assumption, and whereas meanings *per se* are social in origin, meaning systems require the existence of defined social groupings. When such social groupings exist, man is capable not only of evolving specific meanings, but also of integrating these meanings into a system of meanings. Once this is done, such meaning systems have the power to determine what will and will not be accepted as a legitimate meaning in a given situation. Meanings are no longer assigned purely in terms of shared experiences; the demands of the meaning system must also be acknowledged. As a consequence, meaning systems can acquire normative, i.e. governing, character. What might be called the prime sociological insight rests upon the recognition of this fact.

(4) The character of social groups and their meaning systems is determined to a large extent by the underlying notions of unity inherent in their very conception, i.e. the notions of unity which govern the patterns of social contact which give rise to the social groups.

It is to these notions of unity and patterns of social contact that we now turn. Before doing so, however, it is probably useful to add a few words regarding the quaternary character of the intentional frame of reference presented, the multi-level nature of social reality and their implications for sociology, since an understanding of these issues is fundamental to the analysis which is to follow.

It has been argued that the intentional frame of reference relies on four basic intentional dimensions. All four dimensions, however, are not always used. The appropriateness of these dimensions is determined by the levels of social reality which are accepted. At what has been called level I behaviour, i.e. the 'raw experience' level of social reality, only the gratification and power dimensions are relevant. The utility/economic dimension emerges only when social reality becomes a meaningful reality. Similarly, the ordering dimensions emerge only when social reality is seen as entailing meaning systems. In short, at level I, two dimensions are relevant; at level II, three dimensions; and at level III, four dimensions. It is, however, possible at each level to focus upon fewer dimensions than would be logically possible. Political science and economics, for example, both treat social reality as a meaningful reality, level II, but they differ in the dimensions they stress; political science utilizes primarily the power dimension whereas economics utilizes primarily the utility/economic dimension.

Of all the social sciences, sociology tends to be the most inclusive. This is primarily due to the fact that sociology tends to stress level III behaviour, i.e. the meaning system level of social reality. Admittedly, this emphasis upon meaning systems generates an affinity for the ordering dimension. There is really no contradiction in this, however, since it is through its reliance upon the ordering dimension that sociology seeks to incorporate the other three dimensions. As we shall see, it is this double commitment—to meaning systems and the multi-dimensional quality of social reality—which gives sociology its peculiar character.

It is specifically these same commitments which give rise to many of the criticisms of sociology. By focusing upon existing meaning systems, sociological findings strike many people as saying nothing new. But they fail to recognize that there are numerous meaning systems, and selecting the one most appropriate to explain any given act is not as easy as it may appear with hindsight. Similarly, by presenting a multi-dimensional view of social reality, sociology often appears to complicate matters rather than to simplify them. Explanatory accounts which seek to relate all behaviour to a single dimension, be it a gratification, power or economic dimension, appear to get to the bottom of things. However, if social behaviour is as complex as sociology claims, such accounts not only fail to get to the bottom of things, they misrepresent what in fact occurs. This is not to deny the usefulness of such disciplines; it is intended only to stress the utility of a more encompassing perspective, if a more inclusive account of social behaviour is to be obtained.

It is possible to represent graphically much of what has been said in this section with the matrix presented below:

THE MATRIX OF THE SOCIAL SCIENCES

Intentional Dimension Stressed	Level/Modality of Experience Stressed		
	Level I Non-cognitive 'Raw'	Level II Meanings 'Rational'	Level III Meaning Systems 'Normative'
Gratification	1	2	3
Power	4	5	6
Utility/Economic	7	8	9
Order/Ordering	10	11	12

As indicated, the 'Level/modality of Experience' dimension refers to the level of experience stressed, and the other dimension refers to the intentional dimension stressed. Behaviourism, consequently, would best be placed in cell 1; ethologists and naturalists such as Lorenz, Morris, Ardrey and most animal sociologists, would fit best in cell 4; most social psychologists would belong in cell 2, though the more cognitive thorists (gestalt theorists and cognitive dissonance theorists) would better fit in cell 11; most political scientists would belong in cell 5, whereas most economists would belong in cell 8. This would leave cells 3, 6, 9 and 12 for the anthropologists and the sociologists, with the anthropologists traditionally stressing cells 3 and 12 while the sociologists have emphasized cells 6 and 9. (Cells 7 and 10 remain, for all practical purposes, empty though a case could be made for cell 10 as the home for a future science of natural aesthetics.) What I personally find to be most useful about this matrix, is that it clearly shows that whereas most social sciences acquire their distinguishing character from the intentional dimension stressed, sociology is distinguished by the level of experience stressed.

The question arises whether the three levels of social reality and the four intentional dimensions presented are themselves exhaustive. Here I can only argue that, in my opinion, they appear to be so. To support this view I would note that it is specifically these three levels and these four dimensions that social theorists have used, admittedly in different ways, over the years. These same levels and dimensions have also been 'discovered' by most developmental psychologists. We could, of course, hypothesize other levels and other dimensions; similarly, we could attempt to merge them in different ways. From a phenomenological point of view, however, these three levels and these four dimensions appear best to reflect the conceptual apparatus that we use to structure our social realities.

With these points in mind, it is time to turn our attention to the specific concerns of sociology, namely, social groups and their associated meaning systems. At the risk of being repetitive, let me briefly outline the direction in which our analysis will go.

The purpose of this first section has been to present and analyse what has been called the intentional frame of reference and to show the degree and ways in which the various social sciences make use of it. It has been argued that sociology is the most encompassing of all the social sciences insofar as it primarily utilizes level III behaviour, which in turn makes use of all four intentional dimensions, to order and explain human behaviour. This does not mean that sociology is always the preferred frame of reference. Specific types of behaviour often lend themselves better to explanations framed in terms of other disciplines.

In utilizing level III behaviour, sociology is committed to analysing social groups because meaning systems are generated by social groups rather than individuals. All groups, however, are not the same: in fact, in many ways each group is unique. It is nevertheless possible to categorize groups into a number of basic types. The problem is to determine the most useful way of doing this.

In keeping with the prime objective of this study—to analyse the cognitive structures which underlie the more familiar sociological concepts—I shall focus upon the various notions of unity which characterize different types of social groups. More specifically, I have elected to examine social groups in terms of the notions of 'oneness' which govern the patterns of social contact giving rise to social groups and their associated meaning systems. My main concern will be with these patterns rather than with the patterns of social contact which characterize existing groups. There is obviously an overlap between these various patterns. My primary concern, however, will be the genesis of different types of groups because it is these structures which characterize the distinctive meaning systems of each type of group.

Unfortunately, this approach creates certain difficulties, because the types of groups commonly analysed by sociologists, or more accurately, the sociological conceptions of these groups, often deviate from the 'pure' types I will be examining. My reason for focusing upon these pure types is twofold: one, it allows us to locate more firmly sociological reasoning in terms of the underlying cognitive structures of reasoning *per se*, and two, it allows us better to grasp the *a priori* characteristics of such groups and their related meaning systems. In short, by understanding the inherent logic of these pure types, it is possible to show that many of the characteristics of different types of social groups follow from the notion of group utilized.

II
Cultures, Classes, Social Systems and Masses

A. SOCIAL GROUPINGS AND PATTERNS OF SOCIAL CONTACT

While it is possible to define a social group as any aggregate of individuals who can be 'thought of' as constituting a unit, sociologists are generally concerned with groups which act as a unit. This generally requires that the individuals making up the group be related by patterns of social contact capable of generating some sort of 'governing normative systems'.[1] This raises the questions: How do such patterns of social contact arise? How is it that men relate with some individuals and not with others? Why do men select some individuals to relate with rather than others?

There are probably as many answers to these questions as there are relationships. It is possible, however, to abstract some analytical possibilities: (1) People are more likely to relate with those to whom they have physical access; (2) People are more likely to relate with those with whom they share some interest; (3) People are more likely to relate with those from whom they have something to gain or give. In other words, patterns of social contact likely to produce a social group are more probable among individuals who: (1) are physically together, (2) are similar in some respect, and/or (3) are in some way dependent upon each other. In short, individuals who reflect the unity of proximity, similarity, and/or structure are more likely to constitute 'real' groups than individuals who do not.[2]

If such groups are to be more than theoretical constructs, the individuals themselves must see themselves as constituting such units. Such awareness is not necessary in all relationships. There must, however, be a general sense of 'we' if a governing normative system is to emerge. Some sort of recognition of the group as a 'one' is necessary.[3]

Such groups or, as they are often referred to by sociologists, collectivities exist. Furthermore, sociologists have 'discovered' them. In fact, it is possible to characterize various sociological approaches in terms of the types of collectivities and meaning systems which are accepted as prototypes. More specifically, these are (1) socio-cultural/peoples approaches, (2) social class/interest group approaches, and (3) social system/exchange network approaches.[4]

Before beginning this analysis, however, it is necessary, to avoid confusion, to understand what is and what is not intended by this analysis. It is not intended to replace any of the classical sociological approaches. Its aim is rather to reveal and clarify the underlying rationales of these approaches and, in so doing, show how they overlap and diverge from each other. The major theme of my analysis will be to show that the different approaches utilize different cognitive structures in defining social relationships and social groups; these different types of social groups in turn, generate different types of meaning systems. To do this it will be necessary at times to ignore elements of these different approaches and even to oversimplify some complex theoretical issues. There is the added problem of language, since the same terms are used by proponents of different approaches. Here I can attempt to deal with concepts only in conjunction with the approach to which I feel they most closely belong. In light of this, it should be clear that the discussion that follows is not intended to be a substitute for a descriptive analysis of various sociological theories. To understand fully any theoretical approach one must immerse oneself in it.

I am not trying in this book to present an analysis of sociology *per se.* My objective is to present a critique of sociological reasoning rather than a descriptive analysis of sociological concepts, propositions and theories as commonly presented. I am concerned with the underlying ordering concepts and techniques upon which sociology is based rather than with the more obvious sociological concepts which constitute specific sociological theories. There is, of course, a great deal of overlap; in the course of my analysis, I shall have occasion to deal with a number of specific 'sociological theories'. My main concern throughout, however, will remain the underlying structure of sociological reasoning in general. This approach reflects my personal view that it is better and easier to understand and judge a theoretical explanation when one grasps the cognitive grounds of such an explanation.[5]

One last point: In the following discussion, attention will be focused upon the grounds of social relationships which give rise to different types of social groupings. It is, however, the meaning systems associated with these different types of social groupings which give each of the approaches to be discussed their particular character.

B. THE SOCIO-CULTURAL/PEOPLES APPROACH

To talk of a specific socio-cultural/peoples approach may seem to be self-contradictory, since few concepts seem to be more inclusive than 'culture' and 'people'. Sorokin, for example, defines a culture as 'the totality of meanings-values-norms possessed by individuals or groups . . .' The concept of a people has the same tone of all-inclusiveness. Closer analysis reveals, however, that this very sense of inclusiveness requires a specific sense of belonging since, if a culture or a people is to be inclusive, then the grounds for belonging must be sufficiently encompassing so that all whom we feel should belong do belong. In point of fact, while the term 'culture' has been defined in various ways, the persons involved are usually seen, at least in their origin, as physically, i.e. in spatial-temporal terms, 'together'. This togetherness is determined not by the actual distance between the individuals but by physical, spatial-temporal barriers of varying sorts—mountains, oceans, deserts, generation gaps, historical epochs, etc. These barriers do not, in and of themselves, give rise to cultures; there must also be patterns of social contact capable of generating shared meaning systems. For most sociologists, in fact, the term 'culture' refers to these meaning systems rather than to the people.[6]

Once a culture exists, however, it has the ability to maintain itself even if the spatial-temporal barriers change. It can serve as a basis for maintaining its own patterns of social contact. People sharing the same culture will tend to interact with each other. People belonging to different cultures may similarly avoid contact with each other even when contact between them becomes possible.

Despite these facts, nearly all, if not all, ideational systems referred to as culture and social groups referred to as peoples can trace their origin to spatial-temporal barriers of one sort or another.

All barriers are not equally impenetrable; it is easier to cross a river than an ocean. Moreover, people bound together by certain barriers may be separated from each other by other barriers, e.g., people living on a desolate island may be separated by a river cutting the island in two. In any case even the strongest barriers are apt to be bridged by some individuals, while technological developments may eliminate barriers for everyone. All of these factors make the job of drawing cultural boundaries difficult.

Historically these difficulties have been resolved by distinguishing cultures from subcultures, where cultures are defined in terms of relatively stable, impenetrable barriers such as oceans, mountain ranges, historical epochs, etc., and subcultures in terms of more easily breached barriers such as rivers, hills, generational gaps, etc.[7] Persons who move from one culture to another, maintaining some of their old cultural ties while adapting to their new culture, are also often seen as constituting a subculture. This makes good theoretical sense, since the patterns of social contact and meaning systems of such subcultures generally overlap with those of other subcultures within the larger culture. It should be noted, however, that subcultures, like cultures generally, arise as a result of patterns of social contact determined by spatial-temporal barriers of varying sorts.

Determining the specific meanings, beliefs and values of any cultural unit is an empirical task. There are, however, certain theoretical parameters which have cross-cultural applicability. One such set is the four intentional dimensions discussed in Part I. More specifically, the meanings, beliefs, and values of any culture or subculture can generally be organized around gratification/ libidinal, power, utility/economic, and ordering/meaning issues. This is usually done by describing a culture in terms of its marriage/kinship/friendship rules, and its political, economic and religious ideologies. It is true that each cultural unit has its own specific rules and ideologies, which give the culture its specific character. All cultures, however, are similar in that they possess rules and ideologies of the types just mentioned.[8]

The intentional dimensions serve other analytical functions. It is possible, for example, to characterize different cultures in terms of the emphasis they place upon the different dimensions. Some cultures seem to emphasize libidinal/kinship aspects of social life; others, economic, political, or religious aspects of social life. The fairly common practice of referring to cultures as materialistic, hedonistic, idealistic, family-orientated, etc. rests upon such distinctions.[9] In the end, however, our ability to explain why certain persons do certain things requires that we know what the specific meanings, beliefs, and values of the culture are; this knowledge can be acquired only through empirical research.

Although all socio-cultural explanations must be grounded in empirical 'fact', they are also affected by various *a priori* factors built into the approach itself. These factors determine both the appropriateness and the tone of socio-cultural explanations.

By definition 'culture' is a more useful theoretical construct in some situations than in others; if the socio-cultural approach is to work, the behaviour studied must be governed by cultural norms. The meanings, beliefs and values governing the behaviour must have a cultural origin; they must be generated by patterns of social contact which are themselves determined by spatial-temporal barriers. The persons involved must not only be bounded by recognizable spatial-temporal barriers, but these barriers must also influence their patterns of interactions. This does not mean that all persons who share a culture must have contact with all other persons who share that culture and no contacts with persons who do not share it; it does mean that patterns of social contact among the people are both sufficiently specific and encompassing that a distinctive culture can arise. Therefore the socio-cultural approach is more aptly applied to relatively isolated populations.[10]

This does not mean that sociologists dealing with modern societies have not made use of the concept of culture. In most cases, however, they either concentrate on specific subcultures, where the limiting conditions noted above hold true, or focus their attention upon broad, fairly general behavioural patterns governed by correspondingly general cultural norms. Many of these latter theorists are concerned with comparing different cultures which, in turn, frequently leads to an interest in what may be called cultural processes.[11]

It is the tone of cultural explanations which is their most important *a priori* characteristic. This tone is determined primarily by the apparent 'naturalness' of cultures and their corresponding meaning systems, i.e., they do not appear to be dependent upon man. To a large extent this is true, since cultures, in a very real sense, have non-social origins; they are determined by spatial-temporal barriers. Furthermore, cultures, by and large, do not have a social reason for being; they exist because men have been distributed in various physical clusters on the earth. So distributed, they have evolved distinctive meaning systems. These meaning systems have consequently a 'natural' tone; people believe and do what they do because that is what they as members of a given culture believe and do. [12] The question of why is really irrelevant. If one were to ask someone why he or she conformed to a specific cultural norm, one is likely to be told 'that is the way we do things' or, if one happens to ask a more theoretically orientated person, 'that is the way we have always done it'.

The social scientist can admittedly often go beyond historical precedent in the search for reasons. He may find causal or functional reasons for this or that belief or behaviour. In nearly all cases, however, even these explanations reflect the basic 'naturalness' of the particular culture as they seldom, if ever, present human 'choice' as playing a significant part in the evolution of the culture. Cultures are obviously social products; it is just that they don't appear as such. Cultures are rather experienced as 'natural' and 'given', much like the spatial-temporal barriers that give rise to them.

The given or natural character of specific cultures induces their members to believe that the way they see the world and the way they behave is not only the 'right' way, but also that it is the 'only' way. In sociological terms, cultures tend to be 'ethnocentric'. Members of all social groups tend to see the world in terms of the values, meanings and beliefs of their own group. Cultures, however, do not merely denigrate other meaning systems, they, in effect often refuse to recognize them. This is due to the fact that essentially cultures rest on a recognition of a simple 'we' rather than on a 'we-they' distinction. This is not surprising given the underlying cognitive structure upon which the notions of peoples and cultures are based. The persons making up a culture represent a people in and of themselves; they are not defined in terms of others but in terms of their own spatial-temporal 'oneness'. The function of their shared meanings, values and beliefs is to hold them together as a people, rather than to distinguish them from others.[13] In this regard, I might just add, that historically it was primarily a concern for explaining such social solidarity that gave rise to the concept of culture as a theoretical construct.

The emphasis upon social solidarity inherent in any culture is reflected not only in the culture's attitude towards 'others' but in its attitude towards those of its members who deviate from the culture together (because members adhere to it) has been violated. threatening to the culture rather than the particular act itself. That is, what is threatening to the culture is that a norm which holds the culture together because members adhere to it has been violated. There is consequently little gradation in response to such deviant acts. Any act which violates cultural expectations is deviant, be it the breaking of a religious taboo or murder. There are similarly little gradations of punishment since the objective of punishment is to reassert the authority of the cultural norms, not to rehabilitate the offender.[14] On the other hand, this 'black and white' attitude toward cultural deviancy tends to favour mechanisms for including deviancy where possible, especially if the deviancy itself appears to be 'natural', as in the case of certain forms of mental illness. In simple cultures the mentally ill often have legitimate social roles.[15]

The 'givenness' of cultures induces not only the members of specific cultures but also social scientists to accept cultures as natural. This is reflected in the theoretical concepts of cultural functionalism, cultural lag and cultural evolution. All three of these concepts emphasize the 'trans-human' character of cultures. Cultural functionalism, for example, tends to emphasize the way in which the meanings, beliefs and values which constitute any cultural system work in a given physical situation. Cultural lag and cultural evolution emphasize the natural character of cultural change—natural in the sense that cultures change not as a result of human volition, but because of changing underlying conditions.

The predilection of social scientists to accept cultures as natural and given, also affects their attitude towards cultures. For the most part, social scientists have a kind of affection for any culture simply because it is a culture. Any culture is to be valued simply because it is. I am admittedly overstating the case here somewhat. Social scientists do express negative attitudes toward some cultural entities such as the 'culture of poverty' and various 'criminal' cultures. Even in these cases, one finds that the act of treating poverty and crime in cultural terms serves to justify and enhance them. The negative qualities of both poverty and crime are partially offset by seeing them as characteristics of specific 'cultures' or subcultures. Furthermore, even these negative qualities are seen as negative only insofar as the subcultures are seen as part of encompassing cultures which themselves define poverty and crime negatively.[16]

As noted earlier, 'culture' is often used as a catch-all term to include all ideational aspects of a people. Meanings, values and beliefs which will be presented as belonging to other types of meaning systems are, consequently, often treated as 'cultural' by some social theorists. This practice, however, serves, in my opinion, to undermine and weaken the very concept of culture, as it has evolved over the years. It may be argued that defining cultural systems in terms of spatial-temporal barriers as I have done overly restricts the notion of culture. Here I can only counter by noting that historically the concepts of culture and people have, at least in their origin, rested upon such patterns of social contact and the related notion of spatial-temporal 'oneness'. Admittedly, in defining culture in this more restricted manner, I have been forced to ignore issues which some may feel to be integrally related to an understanding of cultures and cultural processes. Most, if not all, of these issues will be discussed later under different headings. They have not been dealt with above because given the main objective of this book—to analyse the underlying conceptual structures of sociological reasoning—I have been primarily concerned with examining the characteristics of the socio-cultural approach that arises from the notion of oneness that is used, rather than with analysing the concept of culture *per se*.

It may be argued that this socio-cultural approach is not really a sociological approach at all. Are there or have there been, it might be asked, prominent social theorists who have utilized this approach? The answer I feel is clearly yes, though the approach is less salient in modern sociological literature than is the concept of culture itself. The works of Sorokin, for one, come to mind. A more recent book which utilized primarily a socio-cultural approach was David Riesman's *The Lonely Crowd*. (Among other recent theorists, I would also list Benjamin Nelson and Ed Tiryakian.) I would also suggest that the socio-cultural approach is the dominant approach of one of the major figures in the history of sociology, namely, Emile Durkheim, especially in his *Division of Labour in Society* and *Elementary Forms of Religious Life*.

Many of the points made above have in fact been drawn from the writings of Durkheim. Quite clearly, Durkheim himself does not begin by stressing spatial-temporal barriers; nor does he limit his analysis of society to what we have called the socio-cultural approach. His concern with general moral orders, peoples and social solidarity, however, indicate his basically socio-cultural vision. Even in his analysis of societies characterized by a high degree of division of labour, his main concern is social solidarity. Furthermore, his account of the causes of the division of labour stresses the changing physical conditions which gave rise to new patterns of social contact. His concern with the physical conditions leading to different types of moral orders and different forms of social solidarity is essentially the concern of a socio-cultural theorist.

C. THE SOCIAL CLASS/INTEREST GROUP APPROACH

The term 'social class', like the term 'culture', has different definitions and uses. The definitions of social class, as those of culture, however, share certain assumptions: (1) The members of any social class are seen to be similar in some respect; (2) This similarity generates patterns of social contact which produce a class meaning system.[17] It is useful to deal with each of these two points separately.

People can be classified or grouped according to some shared characteristic in an infinite number of ways, since they can be categorized in terms of any of a potentially infinite number of characteristics. The explanatory power of any category system is determined by the number and kinds of other similarities. A category system based on height, for example, is likely to have little use since the members of any given category are likely to be similar only in height or height-related traits, e.g. shoe size, weight, etc. Given that sociologists are interested in explaining social behaviour, a useful sociological category would be one which reveals behavioural similarities. In light of our earlier discussion, four characteristics or dimensions come to mind, namely, the four intentional dimensions: gratification, power, utility/economic value, and ordering value.

That useful category systems can be generated by the four intentional dimensions follows from the fact that men use these dimensions in defining their world. How such definitions lead to behavioural similarities, however, is another question. In actuality, this occurs by means of three overlapping but analytically distinct processes: (1) People who are defined similarly may act similarly because they often act in accordance with expectations that others have of them; (2) People who are defined similarly may undergo similar types of experiences which tend to generate their own attitudes and interests; these shared attitudes and interests tend to lead to common behaviours; (3) People who are defined similarly may tend to interact more with those like themselves; these patterns of social contact may generate their own meaning systems which in turn produce similar behaviours.

Of these three processes, only the third is capable of producing a true sociological group, i.e., a set of individuals who have a common meaning system.[18] The first and second processes can produce useful social categories, capable of 'explaining' various forms of human behaviour, but such categories are not social entities in and of themselves; they are theoretical constructs. Such social categories are, furthermore, not specifically sociological in form; they are of equal importance to the other social sciences. Given our primary concern with sociology, we shall not deal with them here in any detail;[19] we shall rather concentrate on social groups generated by the third process.

There are, as might be expected, numerous groups generated by this third process. They are all similar in that their members have some characteristic(s) in common. Furthermore, it is these similarities which give rise to the group. It is because individuals see themselves as similar and because we group things in terms of similarity that the groups exist. Peoples and cultures exist because we group persons in terms of spatial-temporal togetherness: these groups exist because we group persons in terms of similar characteristics.

These 'similarity' groups differ, however, in the characteristics/dimensions that are utilized. They also differ in the scope of their meaning systems. Here we have a difference which is analogous to the distinction between cultures and subcultures. Social groups generated by some common characteristic which possess meaning systems of general scope are usually referred to as social classes; those possessing meaning systems of more limited scope are usually referred to as interest groups. The overlap between social classes and interest groups is often fuzzy, as is the distinction between cultures and subcultures. It is a distinction, however, which still has analytical merit and will consequently be used in this book.

When one begins to talk of social class, one name emerges as of primary importance, namely, Karl Marx.[20] It is, in fact, fair to credit Marx with introducing the notion of social class as presently understood in the social sciences. Even today most discussions of social class can be seen as either modifications or replies to what Marx said on the subject.

Like all social scientists, Marx was interested in explaining social behaviour. He was, however, primarily interested in complex societies. Furthermore, he was interested in the internal conflicts of such societies. With such interests it is understandable that he did not choose what has been called the socio-cultural approach. On the other hand, he was fully cognizant of the role played by ideational systems in governing social behaviour. As such he required a method of subdividing populations which would allow him to make use of such ideational systems. He focused on what we have called social classes.

His problem was to determine the dimensions in terms of which such classes should be defined. He elected to use the following dimension—'The relationship to the means of economic production'. In any given society, he argued, the specific classes which would emerge would depend upon the means of economic production which were characteristic of the society in question. Marx was primarily interested in modern industrial states and their particular class structure. For our purposes, however, Marx's general theory of social classes is more important, since it, rather than his analysis of industrial states, bears most directly on our present concern.

When one examines Marx's writings on social class one discovers some familiar points. To begin with, Marx clearly recognized the difference between social categories and social classes. For Marx, people with attributes in common do not necessarily constitute a social class. To use Marx's terminology, such groups are only *Klasse an sich*—classes in themselves—what we have called social categories. This holds true even if the members of such groups behave similarly. To qualify as a true social class—his *Klasse für sich*, classes for themselves—the members of the group must recognize their similarity and this recognition must itself affect the way they look at the entire world. In short, Marx recognized that true social classes must possess what he called a class consciousness. Furthermore, Marx recognized that patterns of social contact were necessary for the evolution of class consciousness.

Other familiar points emerge when we analyse Marx's central dimension—'the relationship to the means of economic production'. What is actually entailed by this fairly complex notion? In part, it obviously bears on one's economic resources; those who own the means of production are more highly endowed economically than those who don't. Ownership and non-ownership also entail power differences; the man who owns the means of production has powers not possessed by a man who does not own them. Ownership also entails what we have called ordering differences since ownership allows one to establish various rules of action. In short, 'the relationship to the means of economic production' has built into it three of our four basic intentional dimensions.

Though Marx managed to incorporate within his concept of social class three of the intentional dimensions, he did not treat these dimensions as analytically distinct; to Marx, the three intentional dimensions were seen rather as inexorably interrelated. It took another theorist, Max Weber, to recognize, or at least to emphasize their analytical independence. More specifically, Weber argued that social position, rather than being determined by a single dimension (Marx's view), was determined by three analytically distinct components: class, power, and status.[21]

Of these three, power clearly corresponds to one of the intentional dimensions. There is likewise a clear correspondence between Weber's notion of class and the utility/economic dimension, in so far as Weber explicitly defines social class in terms of control over goods and services. [22] There is a similar affinity between Weber's third component and the ordering dimension, though the relationship in this case is less obvious. To reveal this relationship will require some discussion.

Weber defines status in terms of 'privilege' and 'mode of life'. In turn, he defines privilege in terms of prestige. Prestige, unfortunately, he often defines in a circular way by referring back to 'mode of life'. Luckily, in defining status, Weber also introduced other factors, namely, 'a formal process of education which may consist in empirical or rational training and the acquisition of the corresponding modes of life'; and 'the prestige of birth, or of an occupation'. [23] In presenting the latter criteria, Weber reveals that he conceives of prestige in terms of a person's 'right to order', i.e., in terms of our ordering dimension. This is obviously the case with the formal education criterion; the function of education is to allow one to make sense, i.e. order, something. It is likewise the case with the prestige of birth and occupation though here the connection with the 'right to order' is not initially as obvious. When one examines the occupations and families which endow one with prestige, however, one finds either a strong educational component, as in such occupations as doctor, priest, professor, etc., or historically established economic and power resources. It should be noted, however, that such economic and power resources bestow prestige only when they are seen as inherent in the family or occupation. Economic and power resources in and of themselves may enable a person to order the world for others, but a person must be in a position to so order the world for others for a period of time before others are likely to recognize his *right* to do so. It is for this reason that families who have had money and power for generations acquire prestige and status whereas the new rich do not.

In so far as it can be argued that Weber's three components are built into Marx's single dimension of social class, it may appear that Weber's contribution to the theory of social class is not so important. Such a view fails to recognize the full implication of treating class dimensions as analytically independent. It may be true that in some societies there is a high correlation among the various dimensions (i.e. wealth, power and status) allowing us to treat them as a single dimension; in other societies this is not the case. In such societies, therefore, our ability to use social classes to order and explain social behaviour requires that we be able to deal individually with these various dimensions. In present day industrial society, for example, there are individuals who rank high on one dimension but not on other dimensions. We have, for example, the *nouvèau riche* who possess wealth but not status, the professor who possesses status but seldom wealth or power, and the union leader who possesses power but often neither wealth or status. There are, of course, others such as the Rockefellers and the Fords who seem to possess all three. It is interesting to note that such people usually belong to families which have possessed money and power for many years, and this has made possible their acquisition of status. [24]

From this discussion it should be clear that social classes, no matter how defined, are in effect 'interest groups'; the members of any class are held together by various common interests. In this respect, homogeneous groups based upon similarity are different from homogeneous groups (such as cultures) generated in other ways. The cognitive principle of similarity grouping—which underlies the sociological notions of social class and interest groups—leads to inter-group differences as well as intra-group similarities.

Not all interest groups are social classes. An interest group can be considered a social class only when: (1) the shared interests of the members are due to broad economic, political and/or prestige similarities; (2) the shared interests are sufficiently broad to constitute a meaning system capable of functioning as a world view; and (3) the group contains all those who by virtue of the first criterion belong to the group. Interest groups which do not satisfy these criteria because: (1) the shared interests are based on similarities of a more specific sort; (2) the shared interests are limited in scope; or (3) the membership is a sub-set of those who could belong to the group, are merely interest groups not social classes. [25]

Interest groups, because they are organized around more specific properties of their members than social classes, take more varying forms. Whereas a society may have two, three or even nine social classes, it may contain literally thousands of interest groups. Interest groups are similar to social classes, however, in so far as the members of such groups are similar in some respect and in so far as they generate within the group certain shared values, meanings and beliefs. Moreover, the similarities upon which interest groups rest can normally be shown to be dependent upon underlying economic, political and/or prestige similarities. In fact, most interest groups are made up of individuals who come from the same class.[26] They differ from social classes in the greater specificity of the similarity of their members and in the more limited focus of their concerns. The relationship between interest groups and social classes is, consequently, analogous to that between subcultures and cultures.

Any attempt to explain human behaviour in terms of social classes or interest groups requires that we know the specific meanings, values and beliefs of the classes or interest groups utilized. Such knowledge can be acquired only through empirical study. In this respect, the social class/interest group approach is identical to the cultural approach. However, like cultural explanations, social class/interest group explanations are also affected by *a priori* factors built into the approach itself. As with cultural explanations, these *a priori* factors also determine to a large extent the appropriateness and tone of social class/interest group explanations.

The concepts of social class and interest group can be used to order and explain human behaviour only insofar as the persons studied are themselves organized in terms of social classes and interest groups. This, in turn, requires: (1) that the relevant social resources be 'unequally' distributed; and (2) that the individuals involved engage in patterns of social contact as a result of this fact.[27] Again it is not necessary for all individuals to have contact with all others, though this is the case in many interest groups of limited size. It does mean that there must be sufficient class contacts to generate a class ideology. In the case of social classes and interest groups, in contrast to cultures, this entails more than recognizing the common properties and interests of the members of the class or interest group. It is also necessary to recognize the inherent conflict between the interests of one's own group or class and the interests of 'others'. It is in this respect that social classes and interest groups differ most radically from cultures and subcultures, or more accurately, that the pure types which underlie these concepts differ. The sense of 'we', characteristic of social classes and interest groups, is part of a more encompassing 'we-they' awareness.

To give a rather simple example. To say one is an American, a Jew, or a New Yorker (all primarily cultural/people identifications) does not mean that one sets oneself off from 'others' though, of course, it is possible to do so. On the other hand, to say one is poor is clearly to set oneself off from those who are rich.

The 'we-they' awareness inherent in class ideologies has many ramifications. To begin with, social classes look outwards towards the other 'classes' rather than merely inwards. The specific meanings, values and beliefs of a class are usually defined in terms of the meanings, values and beliefs of the other class(es). Therefore a class, almost by definition, must be seen as part of a class system of sorts. Such class systems, however, are by definition conflict systems; the various classes are in opposition to each other.[28] The interests of one class are not the interests of the other class(es). Furthermore, it is in terms of the tensions between classes that the meaning system of any given class can best be understood. It is true that the meaning system of any class may contain elements which do not reflect inter-class opposition but rather evolve from the patterns of social contact which pertain to the class itself. While such meanings, values or beliefs may be used to explain 'class behaviour', they are seldom essential elements of the class ideology.

The combative tone of social classes and interest groups has been recognized by most social class theorists. It characterizes, in fact, the entire social class approach. This is revealed not only in the tendency to see social classes in opposition, but also in such social class related theoretical concepts as 'false consciousness', 'alienation', and the social class view of social change. Equally important is the extent to which this combative tone is reflected in the protagonistic stance taken by 'social class' theorists themselves. I will deal with each briefly.

In discussing cultures it was noted that the members of any given culture tend to reject other cultures. When two cultures come into contact with each other, therefore, there is a tendency for each culture to attempt to retain its own purity. If, as time passes, there is a commingling of cultures however, both the members of the cultures and the sociologist is bound, again after some time, to accept the new cultures which emerge. The new ways may still be rejected by some, but such rejection is generally not due to anything intrinsic in the new ways, but rather to the fact that these new ways have replaced the old ways. If no rejection of the old ways is required, there is likely to be little negative reaction to the new ways. In fact, if the new ways reinforce some of the old ways, they are likely to be accepted willingly.

The relationships in class ideology are very different; they are inherently in conflict. This is because a class ideology is not merely or even primarily what the members of a given class believe by virtue of belonging to a particular class, but the values, meanings and beliefs which serve that particular class. One can consequently look upon the beliefs, meanings and values of a given class and judge them to be in error or false even if all the members of the class have held these meanings, values and beliefs for a long period of time. That is, a class can be characterized as suffering from false consciousness in so far as it can be shown that its values, meanings and beliefs do not serve the interests of the class. Usually such false consciousness results from a class's accepting the values, beliefs and meanings of another class. It is not the foreign origin of the consciousness which makes it false, however, but its content. In short, whereas the 'rightness' of a culture is determined by the fact that it has been accepted over a period of time, the rightness of a class ideology is that it reflects the interests of that class.

The social class concept of alienation in contrast to the analogous cultural concept of anomie reflects this same difference.[29] Both concepts refer to the estrangement of man from his 'proper' social place. In the case of anomie this estrangement is due simply to a failure to grasp and integrate the values, meanings and beliefs characteristic of one's social position; this failure may be due to the individual's inability to integrate these values, meanings and beliefs or it may be due to a lack of integration within the society itself. (The latter is Durkheim's, and I might add, the more sociological view.) In either case, the problem is basically one of not knowing what to believe. In the case of alienation, one's estrangement is due to believing and doing that which is against one's own interests. Man is alienated in so far as he works against himself.

Such anti-self behaviour is not by choice. Alienation, like anomie, is due to social factors. Where anomie is due to a lack of societal integration, alienation is due to the class structure of capitalistic society which forces the worker to work against his own best interests. It does this by first robbing the worker of the profits of his own labour and then using this profit to further subjugate him. Marx argues that this subjugation was more than economic subjugation. The capitalistic system and its associated class structure forces man to adopt a value system which is inherently antagonistic to man's essential humanity. It is this estrangement from man's basic humanity which for Marx is the essential nature of alienation.

I am here obviously only touching on a very complex issue upon which volumes have been written.[30] The important thing to note in the present context is that the notion of social estrangement generated by the social class view of society is quite different from that generated by what I have called the peoples/cultural view. The problem is not the lack of social integration, but the exploitive nature of the class structure.

It is in terms of social class theories of social change that the protagonistic/conflict tone of the social class approach is most evident. To the social class theorists, change does not simply occur, but is brought about by class conflict. The history of mankind is the record of one class pressing its interests at the expense of another class, of 'exploited' classes achieving awareness of their own interests, and of the conflicts between exploiters and exploited. While the actual distribution of resources upon which the class structure rests determines to a great extent the outcome of these confrontations, the relative awareness of class interests plays a significant role in determining the outcome.

Lastly, a brief word about the protagonistic tone of social class theorists themselves. Whereas those who utilize the cultural approach tend to become enamoured of whatever culture they are studying, they seldom feel compelled to attack other cultures. This is not the case with social class theorists, who tend to align themselves with one class or against another class. This is due to the fact that whereas the value of any culture can be appreciated in and of itself, a class value is determined by its relationships to other classes. A culture is, and can be accepted, as such; a class is always striving to survive or to emerge and must either be supported or fought. Whereas the cultural sociologist is often seduced by the 'naturalness/givenness' of the culture he is studying, the class sociologist is usually forced to chose sides.

It may be argued that throughout this analysis of social class, I have restricted myself to one version alone. Many theorists make use of a non-conflict notion of social class, but my purpose has been to analyse the notion of social class in so far as it embodies the underlying notion of similarity as the basis of class and class ideology. Social class defined in this way, I would argue, entails conflict. The non-conflict notions of social class, in contrast, are derivative notions, and are based upon the idea of social groups whose basic identity is not that of similarity, but that of mutual dependency. We shall have an opportunity to examine this issue in more detail later, but first it is necessary that we analyse such dependency groups.

D. THE SOCIAL SYSTEM/EXCHANGE NETWORK APPROACH

Whereas cultures and social class/interest groups rely upon the unity of propinquity and similarity respectively, social systems and exchange networks rely upon the unity of structure, or interdependence;[31] the members of social systems and networks are seen to constitute such units; they are seen to belong together, because they fit, dovetail, or perhaps most accurately complete each other. To fit together in this way the items must be different; this allows each item to offer something to the others which can complete them in some way. Such fits also entail some notion of a whole which governs the fits. The analytical priority of such wholes, however, can and do vary; it is, in fact, such differences regarding the analytical priority of the whole which distinguishes the social system and exchange network approaches. (Social system theorists have priority to the whole whereas social exchange and network theorists generally do not.[32]) To understand these approaches, therefore, it is necessary to grasp the sense of the whole which is assumed in each case. To do this, we must understand the parts that make up these wholes.

Since social systems and social networks are composed of people, it would seem reasonable that such approaches would use persons as their part elements. While certain early system theorists such as Spencer did do this, most contemporary theorists do not. They prefer to use 'social acts'. By and large their reason for using social acts rather than individual persons is that persons are themselves too complex to serve as part elements. Social acts, in contrast, in so far as they can normally be seen both as parts of more complex social activities and as made up of simpler acts, appear to be ideally suited to a system/network approach. Two men running, for example, can be seen as a race; two men talking can be seen as a conversation. On the other hand, even a comparatively simple activity such as eating can be broken down into simpler activities such as chewing, swallowing, conveying food to one's mouth, etc. In fact, social acts lend themselves so readily to a system/network approach that the problem becomes that of deciding which part/whole relationships are significant; more technically put, the problem is finding those activities which can serve as useful units of analysis. [33]

Given that the system/network approach enables one to go from simple to complex activities and from complex to simple activities, the first step in selecting useful units of analysis is to determine limits. That is, at the outset it is necessary to have a clear idea of the smallest, the largest and the most useful intermediate-sized units of analysis. Though there exists professional difference of opinion on the subject, the dominant view is the social action frame of reference generally credited to Talcott Parsons. [34]

In presenting his social action frame of reference Parsons explicitly and emphatically stresses that social behaviour is intentional. He recognized that the form in which this proposition is presented varies from one social action theorist to another; some theorists, for example, prefer to talk of the 'meaningful' quality of social behaviour while others go further and stress its 'normative' quality. In no case, however, Parsons argues, does human movement in and of itself constitute social action; furthermore, I am familiar with no 'social action' theorist who disagrees with Parsons on this point.

If social behaviour is by definition intentional, then a human activity free of intentionality cannot be treated as a social act. This means that while most social acts can be broken down into simpler, more elemental social acts, this analytical process must stop when further division would leave one with acts which in and of themselves are void of intentionality. Eating, for example, can be broken down into chewing, swallowing, conveying food to one's mouth, etc., but one would normally not be justified in breaking chewing down into up and down movements since these movements are not governed by their own analytically distinct 'intention'. (One could perhaps question whether 'eating' can be broken down into 'chewing,' 'swallowing,' etc., but this particular issue need not concern us since we are here concerned with general issues rather than specifics.)

Similarly, while it is possible to combine numerous activities, one is justified in treating these activities as a single social activity only if all the specific and concrete acts involved can be seen to be governed by some unified intention. The number of activities involved, their spatial-temporal dispersion, the number of actors involved, etc., are not the determining factors. Two very simple acts such as John scratching his face while next to him Bill is singing cannot be treated as a single social activity without a governing, unifying intention, whereas the numerous, complex actions of thousands of men spread over miles of landscape engaged in a military campaign may be considered to constitute a single activity.

Knowing that there are limits is different from knowing where the limits are. Given the theoretical concern of this study, however, it is sufficient to know that this approach can be used without committing oneself to a never-ending process of further analytical reductions. There is also no need to specify when the process of integration must end; this again is an empirical question which needs empirical evidence. In fact, while it is nice to know that there are limits and even to have terms with which to denote these limits (the terms most often used being 'social act' to denote elemental units and 'society' to denote the most encompassing units), what is truly needed is some notion of what should serve as our working units of analysis, i.e. the units of analysis that we are likely to utilize in the actual process of ordering and explaining social behaviour. 'Social role' is such a notion.

The concept of social role has a lengthy history; volumes have been written on it.[35] As might be expected, conflicting points of view have often been presented. In nearly all cases, however, it is defined as a complex of behaviours governed by 'expectations', 'meanings', or 'norms', i.e. by ideational factors. Credit must be given to Talcott Parsons for first clearly seeing that, as such, social roles provide us with the perfect working units of analysis required by the system/network approach. He saw that whatever other definitions and limitations we might want to impose on this concept it was possible, in fact unavoidable, to treat social roles as 'level II' social activities, that is as complexes of social acts. That the system/network approach requires these different types of analytical units is clear, given the literally billions of concrete social acts going on at any time. Only if we can, as standard procedure, focus on fewer more encompassing units can we hope to establish some sort of meaningful order.

While a typology of behavioural units is useful, the task which confronts anyone who attempts to apply a system/network approach to concrete situations is deciding which activities go together. It may seem as if this problem has already been resolved since it was previously asserted that social behaviours are held together by governing ideations or intentions. There is still, however, the practical problem of determining whether two or more intentions do, or even can, constitute a unified encompassing intention. This, in turn, requires a framework for organizing the various intentions. Fortunately, certain obvious dimensions for making such distinctions are at hand; I refer to the four intentional dimensions of gratification, power, utility/economic, and ordering that we discussed earlier.

That the four intentional dimensions can be used to characterize social acts and roles is hardly surprising; neither is it very surprising to discover that sociologists have, in effect, done so. Social acts and social roles are commonly characterized as gratification acts and roles, political acts and roles, economic acts and roles and ordering acts and roles, though often not in these explicit terms.[36] While proliferation of social units may appear to complicate matters, it serves in fact to simplify the task of ordering and explaining by providing more information for integrating various acts and roles. The four intentional dimensions, in short, provide a means for dividing various acts and roles into subgroups within which structural integration can occur.

Although the intentional dimensions are useful, they do not, in and of themselves, solve all problems. There is still the problem of determining the nature of the 'fit' which holds these acts together. Again, it may seem as if this problem has already been resolved since it was previously asserted that behavioural units, i.e. social acts and activities, 'fit' together when their respective governing intentions constitute a single encompassing intention. Basically the same technique, which could be described as the 'complementarity of meaning', is used in integrating cultural units. A number of fairly specific and limited ideas can be shown to be governed by a more inclusive idea in terms of which the more specific ideas can be said to complement each other. In the cultural approach, however, it is only necessary to integrate the values, meanings and beliefs, whereas in the system/network approach it is necessary to integrate the concrete social acts within which the values, meanings and beliefs are embodied. Whereas the cultural approach can, in fact must, rely solely upon the complementarity of meaning, the system/network approach, dealing as it does with concrete behaviours, requires something more. The activities themselves must be seen to complement each other; the specific acts must be interrelated.

In relating social acts, ideational factors are still important. They must, however, be conceived in concrete terms which generally means that they are assigned to concrete social actors. That is, when dealing with social systems and social networks it is necessary to show not only that the various intentions fit together analytically, but that they belong together in terms of the actor and/or actors in question. In driving an automobile, for example, the acts of braking, steering and signalling fit together not only because they are governed by the general intention of driving but also because they emanate from the same actor, i.e. the driver.

When one is dealing with a single actor, the job of integrating social acts is not very difficult. It is made much more complex when dealing with a number of actors. Two overlapping yet analytically distinct explanations are possible: (1) the acts may be said to provide the wherewithal for each other's existence, and/or (2) the various acts may be said to be governed by a more general rule.

To conceive of social acts as providing the wherewithal for other acts is to conceive of Act A as possible because of Act B which is, in turn, possible because of Act C, etc. (When two acts occur simultaneously, each may provide the wherewithal for the other.) Such a view, in effect, entails conceiving of social action in terms of both a division of labour and social exchange. The act of reading a book, for example, is related to someone else's act of having written the book; the act of purchasing an item, similarly, is seen as dependent upon someone else's act of selling it, and the act of catching a passed football requires that someone throw it.

While the three examples just given are similar in that in each case acts provide the wherewithal for other acts, they differ in the extent to which the intentions governing each act are influenced and related to the intentions governing the complementary act. In the case of the book, it is not necessary to assume any reciprocal influence. One can assume that the writer and reader are oblivious of the intentions of the other: that the two 'acts' complement each other is due to a division of labour and social exchange resulting from this division of labour. The purchase/sale case cannot be accounted for in this way. There is again a division of labour and social exchange, but here the actors must be aware of each other's intentions. Furthermore, these intentions must themselves be complementary. Admittedly, in the case of the book there may also be dove-tailing of intentions: the author may write to communicate a view and the reader may read to obtain a view. Such dove-tailing of intentions, however, is not necessary as it is in the purchase/sale case.

In the football case one must assume not only complementarity of intentions but also certain shared objectives. Such shared objectives may be present in both the purchase/sale and the book example, but in neither situation are they necessary. In the purchase/sale case, it is possible to explain the transaction in terms of the self-interests of the actors. This is not possible in the football case; in fact, the intentions of each actor must not only complement each other they must be governed by the shared objective of 'completing a pass'.

To say that there must be some shared objective is in effect to change the grounds of the explanation. In the football pass example, it is not so much that Act A and Act B provide the wherewithal for each other as it is that there is some governing rule to which both Act A and Act B are subject. In short, we have switched the grounds of the explanation from type (1) to type (2), from acts providing wherewithal for each other to acts governed by an encompassing rule.

It may help to grasp the distinction being made here by comparing the completed pass with an example of an intercepted pass. In the case of an intercepted pass we would be back to the first type of situation, one where Act A provides the basis for Act B. The interception was not governed by a general rule. In the case of the completed pass—assuming that it was part of a planned sequence of play which admittedly is often not the case—it is the governing rule which best serves as the basis for relating the specific acts.

The distinction being made here may appear to be much to do about nothing. In point of fact, however, it is central to the question of the analytical priority of the whole over the parts noted earlier which distinguishes social system theorists from exchange-network theorists. I will, therefore, at the risk of being repetitive go over the distinction in a slightly different way.

In the three cases presented above it is possible to see two activities, A and B, as fitting together to form a more complex activity M. The nature of M and its relationship to A and B, however, varies. In the book example, M is a 'theoretical fiction': we can talk of M but in so far as it is not governed by its own intentions, it is not, strictly speaking, a social activity. It is an aggregate of two distinct activities: neither A nor B need be defined in terms of M. In contrast, in both the purchase/sale and the football cases, A and B do entail M.

There is, however, a clear difference in the priority of M in the two cases. In the purchase/sale case, A and B have priority over M; (the transaction exists in order that one actor may make a sale and another actor may make a purchase). In the football example, M has priority over A and B; one player throws the football and another catches it in order to complete a pass. In both of these cases, the overall activity, M, requires its own rules. In the football case, however, the intentions inherent in A and B are determined by the intentions inherent in M, whereas in the purchase/sale case the intentions inherent in M are determined by the intentions inherent in A and B. In short, whereas the book case clearly requires the first type of explanation and the football case the second type, the purchase/sale case can utilize both types of explanations.

One important question remains unanswered: How do the general rules operative in a situation such as the football case come into being? The answer is actually quite simple, namely, that the persons engaged in activity M are part of a network of social relationships capable of generating such shared meanings, values and beliefs; there must be patterns of social contact capable of generating the governing ideational properties of M. The division of labour and reciprocal social exchanges provide the bases for such patterns of social contact. In short, just as spatial-temporal barriers and similarity of actors provide a basis for patterns of social contact, so do division of labour and social exchange.

As with spatial-temporal barriers and similarity of actors, division of labour and social exchange are capable of producing different types of social groupings. Only some of these groupings generate meanings and even fewer meaning systems. Furthermore, the line separating one type from another is again often fuzzy. Just as it is often difficult to distinguish a geographical group from a significant cultural unit, and a social class or interest group from a conspicuous social category, so it is often difficult to distinguish a set of social relationships from a social network and a social network from a distinct social system. In fact, if anything, this problem is more acute when dealing with social networks and social systems, because of what may be called the 'ideational ambiguity' of social networks.

What has just been called the ideational ambiguity of social networks is not really a new issue; it, like most of the discussion of the last few pages, was in effect dealt with in Part I when meanings were compared to meaning systems. In short, we are again confronting the problem of trying to determine when a set of meanings becomes a meaning system. In the present case, however, this question is being asked in terms of the more general question of when do a set of social relationships, i.e. a social network, constitute a social system? The reason why this question arises in the present context rather than in our earlier discussion of the cultural and social class/interest groups approaches, is that social contact based upon social exchange is really more than just another type of social contact; in a very real sense it is the only type.

In light of the earlier analyses of the cultural and social class/interest group approaches, such an assertion may appear to make little sense. A review of both these analyses and of the earlier discussion of meanings and meaning systems will reveal no contradiction. Rather it will reveal that what is being asserted here is something which was left unsaid earlier, namely, that social exchange is essential in all social relationships. The cultural and social class/interest group approaches work because persons who are spatially-temporally bounded and/or who see each other as similar are likely to engage in mutual social exchange. Spatial-temporal barriers and similarity of actors therefore, may legitimately be treated as key factors in generating patterns of social contact and hence governing ideational systems; the actual contacts will, however, be based upon some form of social exchange. More specifically, social contacts will be based upon exchange of gratification/libido, power, labour and economic good, and meanings.

What might be called the analytical priority of social contacts based upon social exchange largely explains why the social system/social network approach dominates modern sociology.[37] It also sheds some light upon the fact that, whereas cultural theorists and social class theorists have, by and large, worked out their views regarding the relationship between the social groups they study and the meaning systems of these groups, social system/social network theorists have not. This is because cultural theorists and social class theorists nearly always start with clearly defined social groupings, while the social system/social network theorist often does not. Social relationships, groups, meanings and meaning systems are all entwined. The question of 'what should be studied in terms of what' becomes much more problematic. Should social relationships and meanings be studied in terms of existing social systems and meaning systems or should such systems be understood in terms of social relationships? In effect, social system theorists choose the first alternative, whereas the social network-social relationship-social exchange theorists choose the second alternative.

In light of our earlier discussion, it should be clear that of these two approaches, Parsons' social system approach is the more traditionally sociological in that the rules governing behaviour are seen to enamate from some group; it is in terms of these collective values, meanings and beliefs that individual behaviour is explained. Social exchange theorists, such as Blau and Homans, are more social-psychological in so far as they see the governing rules in terms of the interests of the participants and the processes of social exchange. Even Blau and Homans, however, state that many social interactions are governed by rules and norms which apply to the interaction itself rather than the self-interests of the participants. In short, though they do not begin with social systems, they often end up with them. [38]

Both social system theorists and exchange theorists make use of a wide range of concepts so far not discussed. Most of these concepts refer to either specific types of social systems and exchange networks, or dimensions in terms of which social systems and exchange networks can be analysed. In addition to libidinal/family, political, economic and ordering/religious types and dimensions, we find, for example, such concepts as 'primary groups', 'bureaucracy', 'total institution', 'encounters', 'extrinsic/intrinsic', 'formal/informal', 'open/closed', etc. In addition, there are Parsons' 'pattern variables' which he uses to describe the various orientations possible within social relationships and his Adaptation, Goal Attainments, Integration, Pattern Maintenance variables used to analyse the various tasks which any system must satisfy if it is to survive. [39] While a full understanding of these approaches, especially the social system approach, requires an understanding of these concepts, to examine them here would take us from our main concern which is the *a priori* aspects of sociological reasoning. I might just note that in nearly all cases such analyses would reveal that the concepts rested upon the relative priority of the intentional dimensions and/or the priority of the whole (that is the system) over the parts (that is the relationships). [40]

The *a priori* characteristics of the social system/social network approach rest, as with the cultural and social class approaches, upon the notion of 'we' inherent in the approach. In contrast to the simple 'we' and 'we-they' of the cultural and social class approaches, the social system/social network approach entails a complex 'me-us-them' notion of 'we'. In other words, in thinking about membership in the group his or her own role, i.e. me, is clearly seen; so is his or her relationship with those with whom the individual is in regular contact, i.e. us; and those with whom the group has contact, i.e. them. This 'me-us-them' notion follows from the fact that systems and networks are composed of interdependent distinct parts. Members of systems and networks are seldom governed by the same expectations; each differs from the others. Nevertheless, each generally sees himself as related to these others. Oneself and these others are furthermore generally seen as jointly related to yet others. One's sense of 'we', consequently, is always relative.

This relativity of 'we' characteristic of the system/network approach is reflected in the concept of 'role diffusion', which in the system/network approach refers to a situation analogous to that referred to by 'anomie' and 'alienation' in the cultural and class approaches, namely, a breakdown in social integration. The problem of an individual suffering 'role diffusion', however, is not that he has nothing in which to believe (anomie) not that he believes in the wrong things (alienation). His problem is that he has too many things in which to believe and all are for him proper beliefs; he is pulled apart by conflicting expectations of his various roles. Each role and its associated expectations in itself causes no problem; it is only in terms of the set of roles that conflict arises. To avoid possible conflict the individual must achieve some sort of workable integration of his various roles. He must work out a system of priorities, which usually must be flexible to changing conditions.

This concern for integration is inherent in the system/network approach because it is inherent in the underlying notion of a structured 'one'. The system/network approach requires, however, that integration allow for diversity because it is specifically diversity that holds the parts together. One cannot rely on the homogeneity of cultures and classes without undermining the very essence of the system/network approach. The very unity of the whole must be seen as dependent upon the heterogeneity of the parts.

Social system theorists have, as noted above, traditionally stressed the unity of the whole; they have done this by emphasizing the self-equilibrating nature of social structures. Exchange theorists have, in contrast, traditionally emphasized the dialectical-conflict nature of social relationships. Recently these views have tended to merge together, with social system theorists recognizing the inherent conflict in most social structures and exchange theorists accepting some form of structural equilibrating process.

It is still generally possible if one probes deep enough, however, to find a bias for either dialectical change or self-equilibriating stability.[41]

Initially it might appear as if social system and exchange theorists manage to integrate the 'it is' bias of the cultural approach and the 'conflict' bias of the social class approach. In actual fact they undermine the basic vision of both the cultural and the social class approaches. For even the most committed social system theorist, governing normative systems cannot be accepted as given. It is necessary to show how they work to hold the structure together; the 'rationality' of the normative system must be revealed. Similarly, exchange theorists, no matter how committed to dialectical change, must explain change in terms of the equilibriating and disequilibriating forces within social structures. Cultural and social class theorists admittedly attempt to present such explanations also. They are not, however, wedded to the system/network theorist's concept of rationality. Cultures need not be structurally functional; class conflict need not be explained in terms of the distribution of resources. To the system/network theorist this may seem as pure nonsense. This is due to the fact that to him governing normative systems are to be explained in terms of underlying social structures. To the cultural theorist and the social class theorist, however, governing normative systems are to be explained respectively in terms of an historically given people and the shared interests of a given social class. In neither of these two cases does 'mean-end' rationality necessarily reign supreme.

To the system/network theorist, means-end rationality does reign supreme. It is the touchstone of his whole theoretical approach. It is a theoretical counterpart to his commitment to social structures. It characterizes the tone of all his work. To him, the social world is a rational world: values, meanings and beliefs have specific functions. Whereas the cultural approach tends to breed 'priests' and the social class approach 'proponents', the system/network approach breeds 'professors'. This professorial or academic stance is reflected not only in a commitment to rationality but also in the continual reaffirmation of the complexity of social life. It is also reflected in the belief in the possibility of value-free sociology: (Sociology studies the functions of values; it does not judge them in value terms).

The 'priest, proponent, professor' trilogy overstates the case somewhat. There is generally a little bit of each in every sociologist. It nevertheless reflects a very real difference in the orientation of the three approaches, not only in the tone of the sociological theories themselves but also in the image of man which is presented. The cultural approach presents man as a believer. The social class approach presents man as a social combatant. The system/network approach presents man as a sociologist. My aim has been to show that this is not accidental, but rather a natural outcome of the three perspectives, or more accurately the underlying notion of oneness which characterizes their conception of social groupings.

This section has so far focused upon the three notions of oneness most commonly used by sociologists. In the process, we have examined the Socio-cultural/People approach, the Social Class/Interest Group approach, and the Social System/Social Network approach. In the case of the socio-cultural approach, the notion of oneness was shown to be spatial-temporal togetherness; in the case of the social class/interest group approach it was shown to be the oneness of similarity; and in the case of the social system/network approach, it was shown to be structural oneness. Though the underlying notions of oneness and the resulting patterns of social contact have been stressed, I have been equally, if not more, concerned with presenting and describing the meaning systems associated with these different types of social groups. More specifically, I have been concerned with presenting and describing the *a priori* characteristics of these different meaning systems: the natural, given quality of cultures; the protagonistic character of social classes and class ideologies; and the rational, structural, self-equilibrating character of social systems and social networks. I have tried to show how different notions of oneness give rise to different types of groups with different types of meaning systems.[42] There remains, however, another notion of oneness and an associated type of social group which has so far not been analysed; I refer here to social masses.

E. SOCIAL MASSES

Social masses, our generic term to include crowds, mobs, publics and audiences (again, however, as ideal types) could be called sociological chameleons since they appear to change their basic character so easily. [43]

The contradictory, ambiguous character of a social mass is reflected in its very definition: (1) On the one hand, a mass is generally conceived as entailing the close physical propinquity of its members; on the other hand, as used in such expressions, as the 'mass media' and 'the masses', the term not only does not connote physical propinquity; it connotes physical dispersion. (2) The members of a mass are conceived as homogenous; they are for all practical purposes interchangeable. On the other hand, the members of a mass are generally thought of as exhibiting a great deal of heterogeneity. (3) The members of a mass exert great influence upon each other, yet each member of a mass is seen as an anonymous figure unrelated in any meaningful way to other members. (To summarize, a mass appears to be both a 'one' and a 'many' at the same time. It reflects all three types of unity—propinquity, similarity and structure—and none.) (4) Most importantly, masses appear to be governed by a collective mind or will and, at the same time, to be completely mindless.

These contradictions are due in part to a failure to distinguish different types of masses from each other, and in part to a failure to distinguish analytical types from concrete manifestations of these types. (As noted above, we are here, as in earlier sections, focusing upon ideal types.) To a large extent, however, these contradictions are inherent in social masses themselves and reflect their essential character. Why do masses have such a character? The answer simply put is that the unity of a mass is to a large extent illusory; it is an illusion which serves, however, to generate a type of unity of its own, namely, what Aristotle called the unity of number. [44]

Even an illusion, especially a shared illusion, must have some basis in 'reality' and so it is with masses. In the light of our earlier discussion of types of unities, three possibilities arise: the mass may appear to its members to be unified by propinquity, similarity or mutual dependency (structure). This process may seem identical to that which gives rise to cultures, social classes/interest groups and social systems/exchange networks. There is, however, a basic difference. In the case of social masses, the notion of oneness overrides the grounds for assuming such oneness, i.e. social masses rest primarily on the unity of number rather than the unity of propinquity, similarity or structure. Admittedly, cultures, classes/interest groups and social systems/exchange networks also require that their members see themselves as a unified entity. Their sense of 'we', however, is due to the recognition of their propinquity, similarity or mutual dependency. Furthermore to the members of a culture, social class/interest group or social system/exchange network, the sense of belonging to a group is dependent upon knowing the meanings, values and beliefs of that group.

This sense of knowing what is expected is lacking in a mass. It is lacking because it does not exist. It does not exist because a mass, as an ideal type, is simply a number of people who *assume* themselves to constitute a group, usually because they are physically together. They share no common expectations. It is the illusion that they are a group, coupled with this lack of common expectations, which gives rise to the peculiar dynamics of mass behaviour.

What does one do when one thinks one is part of a group but is ignorant of what is expected? One tries to find out without giving oneself away. The simplest way of doing this is to watch what others are doing and to duplicate what they are doing. This simple act of behavioural conformity generates a variety of results.[45]

The members of a mass, as just noted, do not share any common expectations; they are sociologically an heterogeneous aggregate. It is this heterogeneity which makes it impossible to know what is expected and leads to the adjustment mechanism of behavioural conformity. But once behavioural conformity is selected as the mechanism of adjustment it is possible for members to treat each other as alike since they are now concerned with each other only as agents of specific activities. Simply put, heterogeneity produces a homogeneity of the lowest common denominator.[46]

Behavioural conformity similarly entails that each member of the mass respond to the actions of the other members (mutual influence). Behavioural conformity, however, does not give rise to normative bonds; persons are not related by any ideational structure.

The 'group mind/mindless' character of masses is also a result of behavioural conformity. The power of the sociological approach is that it allows us to order and explain social behaviour in terms of the governing meaning systems associated with different types of groups. The three approaches described previously rely on such governing ideational systems. Social masses do not possess governing ideational systems. Nevertheless the behaviour of the members of the mass is definitely influenced by the mass. This apparently contradictory situation is due to behavioural conformity which forces each member of the mass to act as others do without a governing ideational system.

Despite the lack of governing ideational systems, masses often behave as if they did possess an overall plan or objective. This is not due to the mechanism of behavioural conformity in and of itself, but rather to behavioural conformity in conjunction with the process of polarization. One can find analogous processes in the physical world. Perhaps the most useful example from a heuristic point of view is Ising's model of magnetic bodies. [47]

In Ising's model, metallic bodies are conceived as aggregates of numerous magnetized (polarized) parts (these parts being the individual molecules). Each part (molecule) generates its own magnetic field; similarly each part is influenced by the magnetic fields of the other molecules. The closer the other molecule the more impact its field has. Applied to social masses, this model would picture each person acting in a particular way as generating his own activity field; that is, he would be exerting pressure on those around him to act in the same way. (He is not actually exerting any pressure but rather the others are attempting to imitate his actions by virtue of the mechanism of behavioural conformity.) At the same time, each individual would be affected by the other members of the mass.

With metallic bodies this process can go on and on without producing an overall polarization/magnetism. It is likewise possible for the members of a mass to affect and be affected by each other without producing any overall effect. Such a mass would best fulfil our conception of a milling crowd. It is possible, however, that as a result of outside forces or mere chance, a sufficient number of parts will line up in the same way, thereby reinforcing each other's fields to produce an overall field force which in turn will force the rest of the parts to line up in the same way. When this occurs in a metallic body it becomes magnetized. When social masses are so polarized, they become mobs.

It is the polarized mass, the mob, which is most apt to act in a decisive way; unpolarized crowds merely mill. There is no way to predict how such a mob will act since there are no governing ideational principles. Admittedly, this does not always seem to be the case. There are examples of individuals and/or groups fomenting and organizing mobs for their own ends. When this occurs, however, one is not dealing solely with a mob but with a hybrid collectivity.[48] In short, if a mob has some rational, planned objective it doesn't have it by virtue of being a mob but by virtue of some other type of collectivity which is imbedded within it.

All mobs are not alike: there are differences of tone and mood. These different moods generally reflect differences in intention. R. W. Brown, for example, claims there are four types of mobs: Aggressive; Escape; Acquisitive; and Expressive.[49] Expressive mobs are clearly libidinally oriented; Acquisitive mobs are economically oriented; I would suggest that both Aggressive and Escape mobs are power orientated, the only difference being that in one case the mob has power whereas in the other it does not. That there is no meaning-orientated mob follows by definition.

Though the concept of social mass has been defined here in a manner which is consistent with its normal usage, it would be misleading to imply that there are not professional differences of opinion regarding the underlying logic of such masses. Three basic theories exist: the contagion view, the convergence view, and the normative view.[50] By and large our analysis allows us to reconcile these views. It explains how a number of people who are actually quite different (the normative theory view) can appear to be like each other (convergence/contagion view). It also explains how individuals trying to find out what is expected of them (normative view), end up simply doing what others about them are doing (contagion view). It similarly explains why individuals in a mass do things which as individuals they would not do (normative view).

What, however, of the notions of 'mass media' and 'mass society'. Given that these notions do not imply propinquity, this usage appears to be a language accident. Analysis reveals, however, that this usage is far from accidental; the connecting link is behavioural conformity.

Until relatively recently, behavioural conformity was normally possible only among persons physically together; only physical propinquity could produce a sufficiently strong impression of oneness without a governing ideational system. The appropriately named mass media has changed this situation. Individuals scattered far and wide are presented by the media as a unified group. It is a group without any real ideational system, however. They see themselves as part of a group but a group with no clear expectations or ideational principles. These are the conditions which generate behavioural conformity and 'mass behaviour'. When the media presents a mixed view of what people are doing, it is not likely to generate polarized behaviour. If the media presents the view that people are doing X, it is likely to generate a behavioural fad. Whatever the specific form of the behaviour generated, the mass media is capable of stimulating behavioural patterns similar to the behaviour patterns of persons in crowds and mobs, i.e., impulsive, given to extreme polarities, and apparently non-rational.

Other situations capable of generating mass behaviour are situations in which people are forced suddenly to uproot themselves and situations where traditional social structures break down: national calamities, political and economic upheavals, etc. In such situations a person may find himself in an ideational vacuum and, as a result, subject to the forces of behavioural conformity. In fact, any crisis may lead to mass behaviour, since by definition crises are unusual and hence not governed by usual ideational principles.

In the beginning of this section we referred to social masses as sociological chameleons; they could also be described as the exceptions that prove the rule. They are exceptions in that they are non-normative, non-ideational groups; they prove the rule in so far as the dynamics of behavioural conformity (upon which mass behaviour is based) indicates that men treat ideational expectations as 'normal'. Put somewhat differently, without the expectation of expectations there would not be any mass behaviour. In short, although social masses are governed by behavioural conformity rather than by ideational systems, behavioural conformity itself is due to a general expectation that the mass is being governed by an ideational system of some sort.

F. QUASI AND HYBRID SOCIAL GROUPS

1 Introductory Comments

In the preceding pages sociological reasoning has been analysed in terms of the four notions of oneness inherent in the major sociological conceptions of social groups. No attempt was made to support one notion over the others, though certain strengths and weaknesses of each were noted. Rather, in keeping with the main objective of this book to present a critique of sociological reasoning, an effort was made to reveal the underlying conceptual structures and built-in implications of each approach. In doing so, it was shown that each approach, whatever its own peculiarities, assumed the existence of some sort of governing meaning system. Moreover, in each case it is these meaning systems, or the assumption of such meaning systems, which are central in explaining why men behave as they do. Admittedly, any meaning system, as earlier defined, depends upon some group for its very existence; the sociological significance of these groups, however, was shown to depend upon the fact that they had such meaning systems. In short, in nearly all cases we have seen that the sociological concern with social groups is more a means to an end, than an end in itself.

Historically, however, sociologists have at times attempted to account for behaviour in terms of social groupings devoid of governing meaning systems. A critique of sociological reasoning requires, therefore, that we analyse such groups and their relationships to the social groups discussed above. Other sociologists have tried to combine the various concepts of social groups presented above, and this section aims at dealing with such eclectic orientations. More specifically, it focuses upon quasi and hybrid social groups: quasi because the sociological assumption regarding governing ideational systems is lacking; hybrid, because of an overlap and mixing of the basic ideal types.

It is only fair that I acknowledge here that much of what will be said will be critical in tone. I have been forced to adopt this attitude not so much because I feel the concepts and approaches to be analysed are wrong or useless, but rather because they are often presented in a misleading manner. This should become clearer as we proceed. Whatever the weakness of these approaches, they have a place in modern sociological thought and need analysis.

2   Social Categories

Social categories were briefly mentioned in the preceding section; they were defined as sets of individuals having particular characteristics in common. In contrast to social classes and interest groups, however, social categories do not entail patterns of social contact nor meaning systems. It is for this reason that I call them quasi-social groups. Nevertheless some social categories are used successfully to order and explain social behaviour. This is because certain characteristics, in and of themselves, can lead to similar behaviour. That is, in some cases it is not necessary to have patterns of social contact and governing meaning systems to produce similar behaviours.

As might be expected, the behavioural patterns associated with such social categories are usually limited to behaviours which are direct outgrowths of the dimensions used; the behavioural patterns are due to the common characteristic. The utility of such categories is consequently limited. It is admittedly possible to generate categories based on a plurality of dimensions. Such categories often prove useful in more situations than those based on a single dimension. The advantage of such categories, unfortunately, is usually offset by the complexity of the category system itself. Despite all these limitations, certain categories have proved most useful, as I shall try to explain.

Analysis of the most used social categories reveals that they can be broken down into four main types: first, there are what could be called intentional categories. These are categories based upon a shared intentional characteristic such as power or economic worth. Given man's concern with the intentional dimensions, it is not surprising that he has at times found it useful to use such social categories. We find it useful to be able to talk about the 'rich', 'the powerful', 'the educated', etc. Such categories are, however, in no way inherently sociological, and sociologists as a group are likely to be critical of such categories in contrast to the more truly sociological concepts of social class and interest group. Whatever their explanatory uses, therefore, they need not concern us here.

The other three types of social categories do need to concern us because they are used by sociologists; I refer here to geographical, sex and age categories. I will deal briefly with each in turn.

Analysis reveals that geographical categories, that is people who have a common geographical location, are seldom if ever pure categories. Patterns of social contact and common meaning systems are normally assumed, though seldom openly. This strategy has the advantage, however, of freeing the social scientist from the need to specify the values, meanings and beliefs of the people studied. He can simply. talk about 'Southerners' or 'Californians'. This, in turn, allows him to give more attention to ecological factors which might bear on the people's behaviour. In the long run, however, if geographical categories are not correlated with cultural or class units, they are likely to prove of dubious value.

In contrast to geographical categories, sex and age categories are usually used as pure categories, i.e., as simple aggregates of similar individuals. These categories prove on analysis to be closely related to the intentional dimensions; their utility, in fact, is dependent upon this relationship. What makes age and sex categories useful is not the physical characteristics associated with these categories but rather differences in social resources describable in terms of the intentional dimensions. It is these differences rather than physical differences which account for behavioural similarities.

The young, middle-aged and old behave differently because their libidinal, political, economic and ordering resources differ. The same can be said for differences between men and women. To a large extent these differences are socially determined. There are also, however, biological differences which affect the way these resources are distributed. Generally, the young, the old and females are weaker. This can have both political and economic ramifications. There are also physical-libidinal differences. Males and females stimulate different biological responses. The same can be said for the young and the old. Age also affects one's mental-ordering capacities. Admittedly, all of these biological differences can be modified, if not reversed, by social determinants. More often than not, however, social definitions serve to reinforce these biological differences.

In light of our earlier discussion regarding the explanatory power of ideational systems, it may seem strange that any sociologist would prefer to use social categories. It is not difficult to understand, however, when we remember that ideational systems have traditionally been regarded as being subjective. A sociology based on social categories has consequently the advantage of appearing to some more scientific. The desire to 'explain' social behaviour in terms of social categories is, therefore, not surprising. Most sociologists employing this technique belong to the subdiscipline of demography. Their main areas of concern have been birth, death, marriage and divorce rates, geographical mobility patterns, income distribution, etc.

While demographers are methodologically sociological (they focus on social aggregates), in promoting non-ideational collectivities they, in effect, reject what I would argue is the basic article of faith of sociology.[51] This has implicitly, if not explicitly, been recognized by demographers and nondemographers alike, as evidenced by a separation of demographers from the main body of sociologists. Personally I agree with this judgment—which explains the limited space allotted to it in this study. It would be remiss, however, not to say a few words about the general tone of analyses utilizing social categories.

The social category or demographic approach produces what could be called a sanitized view of social life. The volitional character of social life is gone. Individuals and social groups become statistical aggregates. The foci of concern are behavioural patterns or more accurately comparative rates of behavioural patterns. The future is often more important than the present; man is part of an ordered universe, but has little direct control over this order. The sociologist is no longer burdened with Level III behaviour.

3   Hybrid Groups

Summary.   In the preceding pages I have tried to describe the various ideal types of social groups which make up the sociological perspective. I have examined the socio-cultural, social class/interest group, social system/exchange network approaches and the concept of social mass; I have also briefly commented on social categories. In so doing, I have tried to show that despite their differences, these types share many similarities: all make use in one way or another of the intentional dimensions; in nearly all cases, governing ideational systems or the expectation of such systems play a significant role. Such similarities are not surprising, given our earlier assertion that sociological constructs must be based upon the constructs of everyday life. If there were no such overlap, we would have to question seriously the underlying categories of experience which we have assumed, i.e. the intentional dimensions, meanings and meaning systems.

This overlap may create certain analytical difficulties, however, since different types of groups are apt to arise simultaneously; a pattern of social contact which generates a concrete social group may be 'multi-determined'; it may be due not simply to spatial-temporal barriers, similarity or dependency of actors, but upon some combination of these factors. This, in fact, is likely to be the case with the most prominent concrete groups or, more accurately expressed, it is specifically those groups which are multi-determined that are most likely to be prominent.

In their attempt to combine the various approaches to 'fit' concrete social reality, sociologists have made use of other theoretical constructs. Many of these constructs are reformulations of the constructs of everyday life; this is not surprising since sociological constructs cannot work unless they approximate the constructs of everyday life. (More recently with the growth of sociology, this rule has been somewhat undermined with sociological constructs becoming constructs of everyday life; it is only relatively recently, for example, that people talk about a particular *society* rather than a particular nation or state.)

What then are these constructs? Nothing more nor less than such familiar notions as 'families', 'churches', 'unions', 'nations', 'neighbourhoods', and 'gangs', combined with less familiar types such as 'peer groups', 'voluntary associations' and 'isolates'. For the sociologist, however, these groups have more explicit, often slightly different, connotations from those they have for most people. By and large this is due to the fact that for the sociologist such groups are generally conceived in terms of the various analytical types described above, i.e. cultures, classes, social systems, etc. Families and churches, for example, though clearly concerned respectively with libidinal relationships and meaningful order, are presented primarily as social systems; in contrast, most voluntary associations are generally presented as interest groups. By recognizing the basic structure of these 'familiar' groups, sociologists are able to recognize other characteristics; they can distinguish 'nuclear families' from 'extended families', 'hierarchial churches' from 'democratic churches', 'middle class associations' from 'working class associations', etc. This, in turn, enables them to provide more useful accounts of social behaviour than the accounts of life do.

The power and utility of the sociological perspective is that it suggests quite clearly the lines of analytical investigation which are most likely to prove rewarding. It would be misleading to imply that all common sense notions have unique, universally accepted, sociological definitions. In many sociological works, common sense terms are used in the same way as we use them in everyday conversation. On the other hand, a sociologieal analysis of an apparently familiar social group generally makes use of analytical concepts discussed in this study. If it does not, I would go so far as to assert that it is not sociology. It might be interesting, informative and even clarifying, but it would not be sociology.

Given the theoretical and existential overlap of the various analytical approaches, one might ask why no attempt has been made to integrate these approaches systematically. The difficulty is that any synthesis still tends to give priority to one approach; one form of social contact, one type of group, one type of meaning system is treated as having priority. If this is not done, it often becomes next to impossible to determine group boundaries; all one is left with is 'overlap'. Most 'syntheses', therefore, prove on examination to favour one of the basic approaches, with a good deal of the terminology from other approaches thrown in. Such syntheses have, nevertheless, generated terminological equivalencies and affinities which must be understood if one is to navigate in sociological waters. I will review briefly some of the most prominent of these 'equivalencies'.

Given that there are three basic approaches, three basic sets of equivalencies have emerged: (1) those between the socio-cultural approach and the social class/interest group approach; (2) those between the socio-cultural approach and the social system/exchange network approach; and (3) those between the social class/interest group approach and the social system/exchange network approach. There are in addition certain equivalencies among these types and social categories and social masses.

The intersection of the socio-cultural and social class/interest group approaches. In sociological writings it is quite common to find cultural terminology imposed on what is basically a social class analysis. This generally takes the quite simple form of referring to the belief systems of specific social classes as cultures or subcultures. This is more likely to occur when there is little mobility and when the class is characterized by a high degree of geographical and biological homogeneity. Such conditions are more likely to hold when dealing with the extreme classes of any class system, since almost by definition such classes are likely to be more cut off from other classes. (Cross-class contacts are more likely to occur between adjacent classes; classes at the extreme ends of a class system have by definition fewer adjacent classes.) While one meets expressions of 'middle-class culture', it is more common, for example, to find the upper and lower classes referred to in cultural terms as in such expressions as 'upper class culture' and 'the culture of poverty'.

While such usages can be theoretically justified—the term culture does imply a meaning system and classes have meaning systems— the effect of such usages is to modify the basic meaning of social class. To treat classes as cultures or subcultures is to underplay interclass tensions and to focus attention upon each class in itself; it leads one to see the meanings, values and beliefs of any class purely in terms of that class rather than as a result of its structural relationships to other classes. This can have very decided political implications. The behaviour of the lower classes, for example, is no longer explained in terms of the distribution of economic and political resources characteristic of the society as a whole but rather in terms of the traditions and rituals of the class (now called subculture) itself.

In contrast to the fairly common practice of imposing cultural terminology on social classes, it is quite uncommon to find social class terminology imposed on cultural units. The reasons for this is that cultures, and for that matter subcultures, are by definition homogeneous; it is difficult, therefore, to discover the type of economic and political differences upon which class concepts must rest. This does not mean that cultures cannot be analysed in class terms; to do so means, however, that one first rejects, at least temporarily, the cultural assumption of ideational unity.

The intersection of the socio-cultural and social system/exchange network approaches. The most common practice in mixing cultural and social system terminology is the imposition of cultural terms on social systems; this practice, however, is generally limited to situations where one is dealing with large social systems. It is rare, for example, to find the governing ideational systems of small social systems referred to as cultures or even subcultures. On the other hand, it is very common, in fact almost normal to find the governing ideational systems of large, relatively self-sufficient systems, 'societies', referred to as cultures.

This practice is due primarily to Talcott Parsons, who explicitly argues that the culture of a people is the governing ideational system of the society of those people.[52] Given that societies generally have clear geographical boundaries, such would seem to be the case. The historical or temporal dimensions of a culture, however, differs from that of a society. Different societies can emerge and dissolve within the same culture. Persons who share the same culture may be part of quite distinct societies. This explains why persons belonging to very distinct nation states are still referred to as belonging to the same 'western culture'.[53] Nevertheless, this particular intersection of terminology is so common that it is really impossible to reject.

The reverse relationship, the use of social system terminology to describe cultural units, is not very common. The reasons are basically the same as those given above to explain why social class terms are seldom applied to cultural units; the system/network approach, like the class approach, requires social differentiation, whereas the cultural approach glosses over such differentiation. This does not mean that the system/network approach cannot be used to analyse 'cultural units'; this again requires that the cultural approach be, at least temporarily, suspended. That this can be done is evidenced by the number of anthropologists who have elected to stress social organization in contrast to culture.[54]

The intersection of the social class/interest group and social system/exchange network approaches. The intersection of the social class and system/network approaches has been by far the most extensive and important of the three types of intersections. This overlap is due to a large degree to the fact that the social class approach entails seeing classes as structurally related.[55] One must be very careful here, however, since the principles of such 'class systems' are quite different from the principles governing social systems. Class systems are conflict systems, so that the classes are in basic opposition to each other, whereas social systems are self-equilibriating systems.

One might argue that the proponents of the social class approach should not use system terminology if they insist on conceiving of social structures in such a diametrically different way than do most proponents of the social system approach. Personally, I do not feel such a criticism to be just, since there is no *a priori* reason to believe social structures to be self-maintaining or self-destructive over the long run. There is, nevertheless, a very important theoretical difference which cannot be swept under the rug; unfortunately neither is it a difference which is easily resolvable. The best one can do is to recognize the problem and hope not to be misled when one finds social system terminology being used in conjunction with what is basically a social class approach.

Social class and social system terminology are linked in other ways. The clearest case of such a linkage is the concept of 'status-role', attributed generally to the anthropologist Ralph Linton, but probably most thoroughly developed by Parsons and Merton. In this notion, each role, defined as a set of system-related behaviours, is seen to be associated with a particular status, defined as a particular social position (class), entailing various rights and privileges. So defined, status-roles allow us to look at a person simultaneously in terms of social systems and social classes. There are costs involved, however, since status in this context has a highly individualistic connotation. It focuses on the rights and privileges of the individual and the way in which these rights and privileges affect his relationships with others (basically a systems orientation), and tends to ignore the class origins and implications of these rights and privileges. While status-role does not entail any theoretical conflict, as does the double usage of 'system' discussed above, it is in practice subject to a similar type of conflict. In this case it is generally the social class approach which is 'corrupted', in so far as differences in status are not seen as necessarily generating tension and conflict, whereas in the concept of a class system it is the notion of system which is redefined.

Other intersections: social categories and social masses. The mixing of social categories and social classes is common sociological practice. This is understandable given that both are similarity groups. It is, however, a theoretically unjustifiable practice, especially when social categories are treated as if they were social classes. Social categories are not social groups and to treat them as if they were is to invite confusion.

The danger of treating social classes as social categories is less obvious. It is possible to argue, in fact, that all social classes are social categories. While analytically true—social classes are a specific type of social category; the practice of treating social classes as if they were merely social categories can also obfuscate the social facts. Social categories cannot account for the intentional character of social classes; neither can they account for class structures. While these are errors of omission, they are nevertheless errors of significant consequence since they radically redefine the character of the social situation.

The misconceptions generated by treating cultural units as social categories and social categories as cultural units are similar to those generated by treating social classes as social categories and social categories as social classes. Here again the problem is often not knowing what the social reality is. Does the phrase 'Irish-Americans' in the context of the United States in the 1970s refer to a social category or an ethnic subculture? This is obviously an empirical question. It does not, however, mitigate the theoretical implications of one's answer. To believe that the ignorance of empirical facts can be redressed by theoretical obfuscation is folly.

It is also not uncommon to find social classes, especially the 'lower classes', treated as social masses. This practice, unlike the practice of treating social classes as social categories, is usually deliberate. There is generally an intent to denigrate the class in question. The practice of treating social masses as social classes or as representative of a specific social class generally reflects the opposite intent, the elevation and/or legitimation of the mass. Again it is the empirical reality which should determine how the group should be treated. It is admittedly often difficult to know what the empirical reality is. This, however, does not justify ignorance of the theoretical implications of oné's decision whatever it may be.

G. CONCLUDING COMMENTS TO PART II

Life would be simpler if the various sociological approaches and concepts could be systematically integrated. Life, however, is not simple. If it were, there would be no need for sociology or any of the other social sciences. The value and utility of sociology is that it enables us to cope with the complexities of social reality.

It may be argued that social reality is no way near as complex as the foregoing discussion would imply. In concluding this section, I should like to examine briefly two fairly recent social movements in support of my thesis that social reality is as complex as we have suggested and that we do use in our everyday lives the approaches and concepts, or at least modified forms of the approaches and concepts, presented in this study. The two movements to be examined are the civil rights movement of the 1960s and the women's liberation movement of the 1970s.

The civil rights movement of the Sixties was primarily concerned with improving the civil rights of whom? Negroes? Blacks? Afro-Americans? Initially this may seem to be a stupid question. Don't the terms Negro, Black, and Afro-American refer to the same people? In one sense perhaps the answer to this question is yes. I think it would be more accurate, however, to answer the question negatively. These terms do not refer to the 'same' groups. Negroes are not Blacks and Blacks are not Afro-Americans. More specifically, the term Negro connotes a specific social category of persons having a certain genetic and historical past in common. The term 'Black', in contrast, connotes a group with a specific group consciousness and with definite group interests. The term 'Afro-American' meanwhile stresses what can best be called the cultural heritage of a people. In short, while the individual persons referred to may be the same, each of these terms connotes a very different type of social group.

The women's movement of the Seventies presents us with a very similar situation. What is meant by the term woman? In many ways this is what the movement is all about. In the recent past, it has tended to connote specific social roles: wife, mother, girl-friend, etc. These roles had built-in specific social dimensions; women were expected to be warm, emotional, caring, etc. What is clear is that one did not think of women as an interest group or as a subculture of any sort. One could think of them as a category or as performers of specific roles. Today, of course, this is not the case. Women are now seen as a very powerful interest group.

What is perhaps most important in the context of this essay is the ease with which most people are able to recognize and understand what is happening, even if they don't like it. People know the difference between a social category and an interest group even if they don't use the labels. Similarly, they know when traditional roles are being rejected and new identities are being acquired. They know these things because without any sociological training they are familiar with the range of concepts and approaches presented above. The concepts and approaches belong to the sociologist only in so far as he refines them and makes them more explicit; in the final analysis, however, they are part of social reality not merely the sociologist's reality.

Whatever the complexities inherent in the analysis of the sociological viewpoint presented in this book, it will be obvious to anyone who has read much sociology that the outline presented is, if anything, an oversimplified view of sociology. Various sociological concepts in terms of a limited number of cognitive structures have been analysed. More specifically, I have attempted to show that the various types of groups of major concern to sociologists incorporate various notions of 'oneness', which can be considered to be cognitive structures. I have also attempted to indicate some of the theoretical implications of these various types. We have not yet, however, fully examined the implications of sociological reasoning as so far developed. It is to this issue that we now turn or, more properly, return.

III
The Sociological Vision of Meaning

A. INTRODUCTORY COMMENTS

The function of meaning systems in sociological explanations was examined in Part I. A reliance on meaning systems, Level III behaviour, was shown to distinguish sociology not only from the physical sciences, but also from most other social sciences. Part II focused upon various analytical types of groups capable of generating such meaning systems. An attempt was made not only to describe these types, but to indicate some of the *a priori* characteristics of each. With the exception of social masses, each was shown to be governed by distinctive meaning systems; masses meanwhile, while not directly governed by such meaning systems, were shown to be governed by behavioural conformity which in turn was shown to depend upon the 'expectation' of such meaning systems. In short, this essay has continually underlined the centrality of meaning systems in sociological reasoning.

In spite of this, we have so far circumvented the full implications of this importance. We have not examined what it means for a discipline to conceive of human behaviour as governed by meaning systems. We have dealt with specific ramifications of specific meaning systems, but have not dealt with the theoretical and methodological implications of meaning systems *per se*, nor with the theoretical and methodological implications of a discipline dependent upon such meaning systems. In short, to use Durkheim's and Weber's formulations, we have not fully explored the implications of a 'science of ethics' or of a 'scientific study of meaningful behaviour'. We have not confronted sociology as the moral discipline that it is.

What does it mean to be a science of ethics or meaningful

behaviour? Can or should meanings be treated like other 'things'? In so far as they exist they can be described. We can examine the impact they have on behaviour. Don't meanings have properties, however, which require special treatment? Weber clearly thought that they did; he stated quite clearly that they must be 'understood'. What, however, does this mean? The answer, I feel, is that we must grasp the way ideas are related to other ideas.

To understand how ideas are related may initially appear to be relatively simple. They are related by the rules of logical thought. As Freud noted, however, ideas are related in other ways; they may be related by personal association. These associations, moreover, may be unconscious. There are other possibilities. I would like to suggest a few such possibilities which bear directly on points made earlier. What I will attempt to show is that different types of ideas and concerns favour different ways of thinking. Moreover, these ways of thinking are not necessarily, nor even primarily, inherent in individual minds. They are rather inherent in the structure of meaning systems which, in turn, are part of social reality.

The view that meaning systems 'exist' within the social world does not entail seeing them as somehow free of mind; it rather entails reformulating our notion of mind and its relationship to such meaning systems. Meaning systems are shaped in terms of the cognitive structures of mind, but they are formed within the realm of the social. Individual minds are no more able to grasp their own underlying structures by themselves than we are able to see ourselves without some sort of reflecting device. Man may give the world its meaning but the meaning is in the world not in his mind. Meanings, in contrast to cognitive structures, do not exist first in individual minds. Such minds merely reflect the meanings of the social world.[1]

B. SOCIOLOGY AS A MORAL DISCIPLINE

In the preceding pages I have dealt primarily with two types of basic ideas: the intentional dimensions and types of unity. In analysing the different sociological approaches I have also noted that there are different sorts of social orders; the sense of 'we' and social solidarity of cultures, social classes and social systems differ.

There are, however, other questions which have not been asked. Do different senses of social solidarity favour different types of unity? Do different types of unity favour different types of dimensions? Do different dimensions favour different types of social orders? Do different types of social orders favour different intentional dimensions? In short, do meaning systems, in and of themselves, i.e., as part of social reality, exhibit 'logics' of their own?

What can be said about libidinal concerns, and the effect such concerns have upon our sense of unity and order? Perhaps the most significant thing about libidinal orientations, or likes and dislikes, is that they are often 'irrational'; our likes and dislikes often don't follow logical rules. The objects of one's loves and hates are often the same. Freud summed up this situation in his notion of 'ambivalence'. Mates, children, friends, personal gods are loved and hated simultaneously. As such, libidinal relationships are better categorized in terms of their intensity than in terms of their positive or negative valence. What matters is the strength of the relationship.

Libidinal ties also tend to generate a strong sense of solidarity with those within the 'in-group'; conversely, belonging to an in-group generates libidinal sensitivities. It is not uncommon for individuals who work with others to experience a new sense of 'brotherhood' when they and those with whom they work are treated as an in-group. Ironically, this in-group status may serve to undermine the members' sense of actual relationship with each other. Anyone who has played with an athletic team is familiar with this process. Under 'normal' conditions one is aware of the others in one's team and one's relationships to each. These relationships, however, are normally characterized by little or no affect. You have your job and they have their jobs. When the team is treated as a homogeneous in-group, however, feelings and attitudes change. There is the sense of team 'spirit'.

Team spirit, sense of community, patriotism, and similar group feelings reflect a specific sense of belonging. To belong is to be part of a homogeneous group; to belong is to care. We could say that a libidinal world is basically a world of 'sets'. The basic property shared by members of the set is membership in the set. As a consequence, libidinal orientations seem to generate relatively unstructured situations; similarly unstructured situations seem to give rise to interpersonal affect. This relationship is reflected in the concept of 'primary groups'. It is also evidenced in what often occurs when normal social structures are disrupted; blackouts, Christmas gatherings, encounters with strangers on a train, come to mind. Here one may also note the peculiar character of groups governed by charismatic leaders. The charismatic leader is not expected to be consistent. Periods of social disorder correspondingly often allow charismatic leaders to emerge.

Political orientations are correlated with a different sense of order and social unity. The unifying concern is a concern for structure. This is not to deny that there are political in-groups and outgroups: friends and foes. The concepts of friend and foe, however, are more libidinal than political. The political orientation stresses more who can do what for whom than who likes whom. One need not like one's political allies nor dislike one's political foes. One need not even agree with one's allies on matters of principle or disagree with one's opponents. In fact, as the aphorism well notes, 'politics makes strange bedfellows'. The issue is rather that of mutual influence and the implications of such influence.

In the political view of the world, things normally don't 'just happen'; rather the concern with structure noted above tends to focus upon the interrelationship of one act upon another. In short, there are reasons, political reasons, why things happen. This is reflected in what may be called the 'conspiratorial' view of the world.

This conspiratorial view assumes, however, not only that things don't just happen, but that the reasons why things happen is seldom the reason given. The political view tends to reject 'given reasons', because to accept the given reason normally requires that one perceive men as acting in accordance with stated principles and goals. The political view, however, tends to see social acts as a means of acquiring or maintaining power. As such, to understand such acts it is necessary to know the political deals which lead to the action. To understand political deals, in turn, requires its own sensitivities, since such deals are seldom straightforward affairs. Truly political alliances, in contrast to authority structures, generally have a Byzantine character; A owes B, B owes C, C owes D, but C also owes A, but A owes D, etc.

The political view tends, for the above reasons, to look upon all forms of social solidarity as highly problematic. The world is seen as constituted by constantly shifting alliances. It is the actual structural relationships which are of importance rather than whatever the temporary boundaries may be. There is an important corollary to this; a concern with social structure *per se* tends to emphasize the political character of social action. A concern with structure *per se* even serves to emphasize the political aspects of family life. The same can be said of the conspiratorial view of the world. It is interesting to note how often discussions which begin by focusing on economic conspiracies evolve into political discussions.

The economic view differs from both libidinal and political views. In a very real sense the economic view is less social in character; the social order is governed primarily by material conditions. While the economic view is amenable to categorization, for example, such categories are defined in terms of resources rather than membership *per se*. In-groups are not formed by the commitment of their members but by the fact that they have similar resources. Social structures similarly are due to specific distributions and exchanges of resources rather than the intentions of the participants. This is not to assert that feelings of belonging and intentions are irrelevant in the economic view, but that they themselves are due to economic conditions.

The concern for the underlying material conditions of social life, characteristic of the economic view, leads to a more 'naturalistic' view of social order. This naturalistic view, in turn, favours a more traditional 'rationalism'. Events have specific material causes. The world is governed by logical principles: given X, then Y; if Y, then Z, etc. Events do not simply happen; neither are they the results of fickle human nature or secret deals. The social order with its intentions, beliefs, values, etc. reflects an underlying material order.

As the economic view tends to stress material conditions, the ordering or meaningful view stresses ideational conditions. Social behaviour is seen as governed by principles. As such, the ordering view may be considered the most truly sociological of the four views. Groups are not merely sets or networks of individuals; they have an existence of their own. An existence which can best be called moral in character. Similarly, social behaviour is seen as having a moral character. Social actions can be judged as right or wrong, good and bad. Admittedly, behaviour which in one context may be considered bad, may in another context be considered good. All social behaviour, however, reflects a moral character of some sort.

While the view that behaviour has a moral character rests on the assumption that there are moral principles, the concept of morality generates its own sense of order which in turn affects these moral principles. 'Should statements' have their own logic which differs from the logic of 'is statements'. Moral orders make much greater use of symbolism and analogy. It makes perfectly good sense, for example, when looking at the world in terms of moral principles, to talk of 'evil means' leading to 'evil ends' though the chain of events leading from the means to the end is itself apparently disjointed. People will say 'I'm not surprised it happened' when in fact there was no way to guess it would happen, if it comes out right in terms of their moral scales.

Given the affinity between sociology and the ordering view, one might suppose that sociologists have laboured to understand such logics. In fact, just the opposite is the case. Sociologists have described various meaning systems, noting the most significant 'logical peculiarities'. They have not, however, attempted to deal with these 'peculiarities' systematically. As a consequence and somewhat ironically, sociologists are least successful where they should be most successful, namely in explaining behaviour which is governed by moral principles.

Even the brief discussion of the impact of different intentional orientations just presented invites some interesting comparisons with our earlier discussion of types of social groups. In some cases, intentional orientation and type of group seem to reinforce each other; in other cases, they seem to act in opposition. A libidinal orientation, for example, tends to stress a basic identification within the in-group; as such we might say that it stresses the homogeneity of the in-group. This is consistent with points made earlier regarding cultures, classes/interest groups, and social systems/exchange networks. More specifically, it was noted that cultures, which are themselves based upon spatial-temporal homogeneity, tend to emphasize libidinal/kinship relationships. Social classes and interest groups, similarly, tend to stress the libidinal ties within each class or group. This is reflected in such terms as 'brother', 'sister', 'comrade', etc. In contrast, complex organizations which stress the heterogeneity of their members tend to undermine a libidinal orientation. Rules against nepotism are an indication of this.

The situation is quite different when we analyse the impact of a political orientation. A political orientation, it was just argued, tends to stress the problematic and conflict character of social relationships; as such a political orientation would seem to be favoured by a social class approach. On the other hand if one actually focuses upon political relationships, one is more likely to see the social world in terms of exchange networks. This is due to the fact that political relationships within established cultures, classes and social systems are often not political in the strict sense of the term; they are rather authority relationships. The political relationships have been legitimized by various values, norms and beliefs. The actual relationships are maintained by these values, norms and beliefs rather than by political exchanges *per se*. It is only in exchange networks that emerging structures are likely to be dependent upon purely political factors. This, in part, I feel, explains why exchange theorists such as Blau tend to be more concerned with power than sociologists favouring other approaches. In short while a social class approach would seem to favour a political orientation, a political orientation seems to favour a system/exchange network approach.

The economic orientation presents us with what is apparently the reverse situation to that presented by political orientation. In so far as it emphasizes the division of labour and means/end rationality, it would seem most appropriate to the system/network approach. On the other hand, economic concerns in and of themselves would seem to favour the social class approach. Admittedly, the social class approach has a system aspect to it but, as noted, class systems tend to emphasize conflict rather than complementarity. In short, whereas the political orientation seems to favour the system approach but to be favoured by the class approach, the economic orientation seems to favour the class approach but to be favoured by the system approach.

While it is somewhat unclear why such shifts in orientation should occur, it is interesting to note that such shifts are consistent with certain important historical developments. Socialism, for example, initially emerged as an economic ideology. Admittedly, there were always political objectives. These political objectives were seen, however, as necessary to achieve economic ends, namely, the more equitable distribution of economic resources. In practice, however, socialism has proved to be more a political movement than an economic movement. The infra-structure of most socialistic states is the party, not the economy. In contrast, western 'democracies' emerged emphasizing man's political rights. The stress was upon checks and balances of political power. In practice, however, such division of power has been institutionalized within the economic systems of these societies. The political influence of individual citizens has in effect become equated with their economic resources. In light of points made earlier this is really not surprising. One may start with what one considers to be an economic conflict of interests, but a conflict orientation in itself leads to a political orientation. Similarly, one may start with the objective of establishing a political system of checks and balances, but any system intentionally based upon self-equilibrating social exchange will tend to rely upon economic exchanges.

Of the various intentional orientations, the ordering orientation is the most difficult to deal with. To a large extent this is due to the fact that an ordering orientation can be grafted onto any of the other three intentional orientations. In its pure form, however, an ordering orientation stressed principles of universal morality. As such, it is most compatible with orientations which stress the basic sameness of the members of the society, or group. It is consequently most compatible with what we have called the cultural approach. This is reflected in the emphasis given to 'religion' in most cultural studies. The concern for universal ordering principles is decidedly less in most complex societies. In even the most complex and heterogeneous societies persons discuss such principles, but analysis usually reveals that such principles are justified in terms of specific political, economic, and/or organizational needs. Individuals concerned with organizing their lives in terms of 'pure principles' generally tend to separate themselves from the general society. Most communes, whatever their other differences, tend to exhibit such a concern for pure principles.

My treatment of the issues just discussed is admittedly superficial. My objective was not, however, to analyse exhaustively the relationships among the various orientations discussed. It was rather to indicate the types of analyses which, I feel, are required if sociology is to fulfil its promise. Unfortunately, it is specifically this type of analysis which has been most lacking. The reason, as I see it, is two-fold: first, there has been a general failure to treat meaning systems inherent in social reality; secondly, there has been a failure to emphasize the moral character of most meaning systems.[2]

There have been exceptions to these general trends, especially the first. Theorists in the 'sociology of knowledge', and more recently ethnomethodologists have all stressed, in their own way, the need to analyse meaning systems in and of themselves. The anthropologist Claude Levi-Strauss has made a similar point.[3] The tendency has been, however, to recognize the moral character of only those meaning systems which are explicitly moral orders. This is doubly disturbing, because if sociology has anything to say about meaning systems it is that they are all moral in character; they are the means whereby men as members of different groups decide what should and should not be done.

Meaning systems convey more than meanings; they provide the very bases for social life and the criteria for 'right' action. Furthermore, this moral character pertains to meaning systems which are not ostensibly moral. To treat meaning systems as only in individual minds or to limit one's attention to explicit moral orders is to obfuscate the basic soiological insight. It may even serve to negate it. The moral orders of the mundane world are merely the tips of icebergs; we can describe these tips but such accounts will not allow us to understand the icebergs in their totality. Similarly phenomenological and psychological reductionism may serve to clarify our understanding of meaning systems as they exist in individual minds, but neither approach can account for an 'intersubjectivity' capable of supporting our sense of the social. If sociology is *sui generis*, which I believe it is, it must evolve its own methods for dealing with its own problems.

It is one thing to recognize a problem and another thing to resolve it. In light of our analysis, I would suggest that the intentionality and underlying sense of unity of a meaning system offer a suitable beginning. So I should like to examine briefly four concepts which appear to reflect such conceptual nexuses. These concepts are Loyalty, Duty, Justice, and Righteousness.

Loyalty, duty, justice and righteousness are all moral concepts in that they favour specific types of social behaviour, or more accurately, specific rules for social behaviour. All set certain principles which should govern human interaction. These principles, however, are not the same; often, in fact, they may be in conflict. Such conflict is due to the fact that these concepts assume different types of social solidarity. Loyalty assumes solidarity based upon homogeneity and libidinal diffusion; duty assumes solidarity based upon hierarchical structure and power; justice assumes solidarity based upon social differentiation and social utility; righteousness assumes solidarity based upon normative principles and a sense of social order.

Let us look at some concrete though hypothetical examples. Assume that Mr Jones must select one individual from a number of applicants for a desirable job or assignment. Let us further assume the following: (1) one of the applicants is a close relative; (2) the job requires specific skills; (3) his boss has indicated to him the person that he would like. Whom should Mr Jones select? Does family loyalty require that he select his cousin? Does duty to his boss require that he favour his boss's candidate? Should he select the person most qualified? Or should he perhaps select the person most in need of the job?

In light of the limited information given, I am sure that there would be a wide range of opinions as to what Mr Jones should do. If we further restrict the situation, however, a greater degree of consensus is likely. If we assume a business organization setting, for example, I would guess that most persons would feel that Mr Jones should hire the person most qualified, though in point of fact he might favour his boss's candidate. In contract, if Mr Jones is operating in a strictly political situation—he is selecting a delegate for some political committee—more persons, I would guess, would feel that he should favour his boss's candidate. On the other hand, there are situations where Mr Jones may feel that he should favour his cousin. I have in mind situations in which he would be hiring day labourers from an ethnically homogeneous group. I can also imagine situations—a public works project—in which Mr Jones may feel that he should hire the person most in need of the job.

Different social situations favour different choices because the social grounds for morality—social solidarity—itself varies. When social solidarity is based upon family, ethnic or class homogeneity, family, class or ethnic loyalty is moral. When social solidarity is based upon a political hierarchy, fealty is moral. When social solidarity is based upon a division of labour, meritocracy is moral. When social solidarity is based upon general 'moral' principles, acts of principle, i.e., righteous acts, are moral. In contrast, when social solidarity is based upon family, ethnic or class homogeneity, fealty to an outsider, universal justice and acts of abstract principle may be seen as immoral. Loyalty, similarly, may be considered immoral where solidarity is based upon a division of labour, political stratification or universal principles.

The grounds for social solidarity in any concrete situation may be complex; it may entail both homogeneity and political stratification or political stratification and a division of labour. Furthermore, the primary ground for solidarity is often not what it initially appears to be. Political clubs, for example, are often held together by loyalty and homogeneity of members rather than by a political hierarchy. Economic institutions are often held together by a political hierarchy rather than by a division of labour. Voluntary associations are often held together by a division of labour rather than by homogeneity and loyalty. To complicate things further the grounds for solidarity of any group may themselves change over time, giving rise to a new sense of morality. It is only by tackling these problems head on that sociology can hope to be true to its own vision of human behaviour. Sociology must do more than describe what men do; it must even do more than describe the meanings, values and beliefs which govern social behaviour. It must seek to explain the underlying rationales of these meaning systems; it must reveal the rules and 'logics' inherent in these different meaning systems. We might say in fact that this is one of, if not the, central task of sociology.[4]

The first step, of course, is to recognize that there are different types of rationalities and moral orders. Unfortunately, this fact is often ignored, even in the best of sociological works. In support of this assertion I should like to examine briefly a number of sociological classics and issues of sociological concern. My purpose in each case will be to indicate some of the benefits to be gained by recognizing these different types of rationalities and moral orders as well as some of the costs entailed by a failure to do so.

COMMENTS ON SOME SOCIOLOGICAL STUDIES AND ISSUES

The following comments are not meant to be general critiques of the works cited. In each case I have dealt only with certain aspects of the studies which bear on the general question of the theoretical orientation embodied in the work and the extent to which such orientation lead these authors to see certain things and not others. Each of these studies is much richer than would be deduced from my limited treatment of them. In most cases, there exists a substantial literature of analyses, most of which I have made no reference to.

The comments presented below are not meant to refute nor negate the basic insights and conclusions of the studies commented upon. Each is a sociological classic which deserves the praise that it has received. My purpose is rather to point out the need to be constantly sensitive to the vagaries of any moral order and, more specifically, to the relationship between different types of moral orders and rationality. My objective in each case is to reveal how any given theoretical orientation may limit our ability to understand some behaviour while it explains other behaviour.

All of the authors discussed below were successful in explaining certain behaviours by revealing a rationality which previously was only dimly appreciated. Whyte showed that the inhabitants of 'Cornerville' were not governed purely by tradition; much of their behaviour could be better explained in terms of the rules of give and take characteristic of social systems. Stouffer *et al.* similarly revealed that personal adjustment and commitment to the war was based on much more than 'patriotism'. Bettleheim demonstrates the power of the psychoanalytical perspective, while Mills shows how economic changes have redefined the political reality of the American middle class. Weber, in his analysis of the Protestant Ethic and the Spirit of Capitalism, meanwhile achieved what can only be called a revolution in the manner in which we look upon the relationship between different types of meaning systems.

Despite their accomplishments, it is my opinion that each also failed to recognize the limitations of their own perspective. It is to highlight the relationships between different theoretical viewpoints, different types of moral orders, and different types of rationalities that these comments are presented.

1. Street Corner Society *by W. F. Whyte*[5]

The first study which I should like to comment on is Whyte's *Street Corner Society*; more specifically I should like to examine Whyte's treatment of what he calls the 'racketeers'.

Whyte's study is set in the Italian North End of Boston during the depression years of 1937–1940. His primary concern is the political structure of the North End. Though he focuses his study on the informal gangs of this area he spends a good deal of time analysing the role of the racketeers. He is particularly interested in explaining the apparent legitimacy of these racketeers in the Italian community. He concludes that the racketeers are accepted within the community because they fulfil important political and economic functions. He shows how the racketeers provide a link between the community and the political organs of the city. He shows how the racketeers provide jobs. In short, he provides a system-exchange theory explanation for their legitimacy.

Whyte's analysis is probably correct in as far as it goes. What he fails to convey to the reader, however, is that the racketeers of the North End were probably not simply persons involved in organized crime, but also Mafiosi and as such titled to a degree of 'cultural' legitimacy. To treat racketeers in an Italian, heavily Sicilian, community in the 1930s simply as racketeers would appear to ignore the total picture. They were probably not accepted merely because they provided jobs and political influence. Their political power was probably due as much to the fact that they were seen as legitimate within the community, as that their legitimacy was due to their political power. Similarly, the fact that they provided economic assistance may have been due as much to the traditional role of the Mafiosi as it was to the economic rationality of organized crime. This is supported by the fact that though racketeers are common to most slum communities they do not possess the same legitimacy in all such communities. (In this context, the correlation between acceptance of black racketeers in black communities and the growth of black consciousness is worth noting.)

Whyte is probably correct in saying that much of the respect given the racketeers was based on some sense of justice; they (the racketeers) deserved respect because they provided political in-

fluence and economic benefits. This respect could well be based
equally upon the fact that the Mafiosos were the traditional
spokesmen for the community. There existed a blood bond between
the members of the community and the racketeers; a bond which
entailed loyalty and duty, as much if not more than distributive
justice.

It is interesting to note in this regard that although Whyte
himself stresses one type of social relationship, his study clearly
reveals that the citizens of the North End were aware of the
complex nature of such relationships. In the section on 'Politics
and the Social Structure', for example, Whyte writes, 'Political
speeches in Cornerville cover five main points: the racial appeal,
the class appeal, the personal appeal, a statement of qualifications
for office, and the statement of the candidate's political
strength.'[6] In the light of the points made above, we would have to
conclude that the politicians of 'Cornerville' were pretty good
sociologists.

2. The American Soldier *by Stouffer* et al.[7]

The American Soldier covers such a wide range of data that it will
be possible for me to touch on only a few items here. These will, I
hope, be sufficient to support my major thesis that the authors of
this study failed to explain their data adequately because they relied
on a too-limited notion of social legitimacy. More specifically, the
authors attempt to explain 'morale' almost exclusively in terms of
soldiers' sense of fair play and justice. While such a sense of fair
play and justice can explain many of their findings it cannot explain
all of them. In fact, an attempt to do so can and, I feel, does lead to
a good deal of misinterpretation of the data. I will briefly analyse
three sets of findings to support this claim.

The authors note that the more highly educated soldier tended to
be more critical of the army way of doing things, least convinced of
the importance of what he was doing and least satisfied with his
status and job; on the other hand, he also showed the most personal commitment to the war and tended more frequently to say
that he was in good spirits.[8] This apparently contradictory situation
is explained by the authors by observing that the more highly
educated soldier had a better chance for promotion.[9] This being so,

they argue, he was more positively disposed towards the army.

This explanation, however, makes little sense since if he treated his chance for promotion as offsetting the other injustices he felt, it is doubtful whether he would be so negative towards the army way of doing things. Furthermore, there is little reason to believe that military promotion would have the positive impact that the authors attribute to it. It is much more reasonable to argue, I believe, that the more highly educated soldier was committed to the war not because of the 'deal' he was getting, i.e. that he was being treated justly, but because he saw the war as necessary and morally correct.

A similar somewhat contradictory situation seems to emerge when we analyse the data bearing on soldiers 'Absent Without Official Leave'.[10] The AWOLs tended to be less highly educated, despite the fact that it was specifically the less educated soldier who tended to be most positively disposed to the army. Admittedly the AWOLs also tended to be younger and the younger soldiers were more critical of the army. On the other hand the younger soldiers showed more personal commitment and a greater willingness to serve. Again, the authors attempt to explain this by noting that the younger, less educated soldier had less chance for promotion.

The background data on AWOLs, however, also shows that as a group they tended to have a history of truancy and non-sociability. It is hard to imagine that such individuals would have expected to be promoted in the army. It is much more reasonable to assume that many of these soldiers expected the army to take them in. By becoming soldiers they expected to become one of the boys. This in part could explain why the percentage of AWOLs who had enlisted was the same as for the army in general. It is also consistent with the responses given by those who felt they should not have been drafted (they were needed by dependents and their health was not good) and the data indicating higher rates of truancy and previous asocial behaviour patterns. In summary the findings seem to support the thesis that the AWOLs were unhappy in the army not so much because they felt it to be unjust, but more because they did not feel that the army really cared enough about them as individuals. In short, they did not feel like one of the boys.

One of the most interesting findings of the American Soldier study was that while combat soldiers tended to feel least satisfied with many aspects of their army careers, they tended to have more favourable attitudes towards their officers.[11] Here again, the authors try to explain this in terms of perceived justice in the distribution of rewards. They argue that in combat, officers received fewer privileges as compared to the enlisted man than in non-combat areas. Again their explanation is problematic at best, since the life and death power of officers in combat is much greater than anywhere else. Furthermore, despite their findings, it is a well-known fact that a much higher percentage of officers are killed by their own men in combat than in non-combat areas. A more reasonable explanation of their findings would be therefore that in combat, social solidarity and survival is much more dependent upon the chain of command. In combat inequality becomes irrelevant; what is important is keeping the unit together and to do this autocratic power is often necessary. You either accept your leader and follow him or replace him.

Without doubt many of the attitudes of most of the soldiers in most situations were governed by a sense of fair play and justice which operated in civilian life. Given the character of American society before the war, this would make good sense. America was a large, heterogeneous, industrial society; as such it was and still is a society held together primarily by a morality of justice. The findings of *The American Soldier* would indicate, however, that for some individuals and in some situations the moralities of righteousness, loyalty and duty superseded that of justice.

3. The Informed Heart *by Bruno Bettelheim*[12]

Bruno Bettelheim's study of life in German concentration camps is a fascinating example of how one's theoretical viewpoint may cause one to misinterpret the acts of others. Without doubt, Bettelheim's study contains numerous insightful observations regarding human behaviour under conditions of stress. His psychoanalytical orientation, however, also prohibited him from understanding and appreciating much that he observed. More specifically, he failed to grasp the political legitimacy of much that he observed.

Given Bettelheim's middle-class origins, this is not so surprising. As a member of the Austrian middle class, Bettelheim's concept of morality was one which entailed family and group loyalty, a sense of justice, and an adherence to various moral principles. Political morality, i.e. duty to political comrades and a political ideology, was foreign to him. He tended, in fact, to treat such moraltiy as pathological in so far as it placed limits on one's own autonomy. This is reflected in much that Bettelheim has to say about the political prisoners. In some cases, Bettelheim's misinterpretations are due to his own political naivety; in other cases, it is due to his theoretical bias.

Bettelheim makes a great deal about what he considered to be the identification of the old prisoners with the SS.[13] He notes that some prisoners aped the brutality of the SS guards. He also notes that some among the prisoner elite scrounged SS-type uniforms. He further notes that the political prisoners frequently played a game, which entailed hitting each other, that the SS guards played. What he fails to note is that many prisoners, especially at Buchenwald, were neither political prisoners nor Jews but simply hardened criminals. That these prisoners would act sadistically is not surprising.[14] That many of the old political prisoners scrounged old uniforms had little to do with an attempt to identify with the SS. Originally, 1936, all prisoners were clothed in old uniforms. These uniforms were much superior to the new camp uniforms which were introduced in 1938. The decision on the part of most of the old political prisoners to use these uniforms had nothing to do with identifying with the SS; it was a question of survival. Finally, the hitting game Bettelheim refers to was an old 'boy-scout type' game which most of the political prisoners had played before they ever came to the concentration camp. Given Bettelheim's background it is not surprising that he was ignorant of these facts; on the other hand, this ignorance led him to some dubious conclusions.

More important than the oversights mentioned above, is Bettelheim's failure to understand what life in the camp meant to the political prisoners. To them, the concentration camp was not an aberration of normal political life to the same degree as it was to the non-political prisoners such as Bettelheim. They saw the concentration camps as a natural outgrowth of Nazi Germany. Bettelheim makes much out of the fact that the old political prisoners were concerned only with life in the camp; he says they had no concern with what went on outside.[15] What he fails to understand is that, to the political prisoner, what went on in the camp was directly related to what went on outside the camp. It was only the non-political prisoner who saw the camp as an aberration from normal 'reality'. To the non-political prisoner like Bettelheim normal life meant family, occupation, speeches by Roosevelt, etc. To the political prisoner, normal life entailed political intrigues and political shifts of which changes in the camp personnel were a sign. Bettelheim was apparently completely ignorant of the continued contacts between persons in the camps and those outside.[16]

Bettelheim errs most grievously, however, in his failure to understand the morality of power. To Bettelheim, the old political prisoners who sought to gain and maintain power, did so for purely selfish, often pathological, reasons. He criticizes quite severely their ability to ignore those who were not part of their group and to be hard on those who deviated from their rules. He gives as one example the 'brutality' of an old timer who beat up a new prisoner who refused to say who had stolen his bread.[17] He sees this prisoner's refusal to tell as a sign of his own personal integrity and courage. What he fails to see is that such 'integrity' was in fact amoral in the camp. The prime objective of any moral system is the survival of the group. In the concentration camp, to the political prisoners the only morality that worked was a political morality.

Bettelheim, in effect, proves this with an account of one of his personal experiences, though he chooses, I feel, to misinterpret it. He tells the story of how he managed to receive medical treatment at a time when the SS was refusing to treat most cases.[18] He describes how the other prisoners pleaded for care and how they mentioned previous service in the first world war, etc. They were all refused care. He, in contrast, simply said that he could not work with his frostbitten hands and left it to the guard to judge whether or not this was the case. Bettelheim claims that the guard allowed him to be treated because he had not treated the guard in a stereotyped manner, projecting on to him all sorts of qualities that he, the guard, did not possess. What he fails to note is that he also acted according to the rules, stressing the work-related nature of his injury, and treated the guard as a legitimate authority figure. He adds that he was allowed further treatment because he did not cry out in pain when he was treated.

Bettelheim argues that he was successful because he responded to the given situation rather than attempting to work out a plan in advance. He is, in fact, critical of his fellow prisoners who attacked him because he wouldn't tell them what he planned to say to the guard. Without doubt, his psychoanalytic training probably was of some help in this situation. More important, however, was the fact that he acted according to the rules and in so doing appeared to justify these rules. Ironically, he does not feel that his ability to endure pain without crying was an act of identification with the norms of the SS, nor that his failure to share his plan with his fellow prisoners was a selfish act. (If there ever was a rationalization, it is his claim that he had no plan. To tell the other prisoners that he would respond to the situation as it was without specifying the need not to threaten the authority of the guard, is like giving a recipe without the main ingredient.)

Bettelheim uses his own experience with the guard to support his main thesis, that to survive one had to remain an autonomous being.[19] In fact, of course, the manner in which he survived in this particular instance entailed submerging his own autonomy; he presented himself not as an individual deserving of treatment but as a worker whose hands were injured. Admittedly, he was aware of what he was doing and acted the way he did in order to survive. When others did similar things, however, he saw them as actively seeking anonymity rather than autonomy. During morning roll call, it was common for prisoners to attempt to find a place somewhere in the middle of the group where they would not be seen. Though he gives numerous reasons why such positions were desirable, he sees such behaviour as a form of childish regression. Given that these positions were fought over, I would suggest that only those prisoners with a very strong sense of self ever made it to the centre.

Bettelheim's problem is that he fails to appreciate man as a socio-political being. Concern for power and political morality is for Bettelheim—and for many if not most psychoanalytically trained persons—in its very nature pathological. In the best of all possible worlds this may in fact be the case; in the world in which we live, however, political hierarchies not only exist but are seen as legitimate. To understand man, therefore, it is necessary to treat these political structures seriously.[20]

4. White Collar *by C. Wright Mills*[21]

Mills in his study *White Collar* focuses upon the 'new middle class' and the political ramifications of this new class for American society at large. He tries to show how changes in the economic structure of the society have generated shifts in political power. In so doing, Mills adopts a fairly traditional Marxian approach. Mills, however, no doubt as a result of the works of men like Weber and the age in which he lived, treats economic and political structure as more analytically independent of each other than does Marx. Unfortunately he fails to follow through on the full implications of this distinction. In fact, I would argue, that he ends up defining power in economic terms. As a result he tends to interpret certain economic acts as political acts and to ignore certain crucial non-economic political facts.[22] To support this assertion, it is necessary to review briefly Mills' thesis.

Mills argues that the 'political ideology' of earlier laissez-faire capitalism with its emphasis upon entrepreneurship, free competition, production, small holdings, etc. has given way to a new ideology of big business which emphasizes managerial expertise, monopolistic control, consumption, sales, bureaucracy, etc. This ideological shift has brought with it a redistribution of power where fewer and fewer people located at the top of these new large organizations now hold the power which previously was shared by those lower in the political hierarchy. According to Mills, authority has given way to the power of manipulation. As a consequence, the new middle class is more impotent and alienated than the old middle class.

To a large extent what Mills has to say is correct. What he fails to recognize is that these 'political ideologies' of the new middle class are really not political ideologies; they are rather economic ideologies, in so far as they serve primarily to ensure economic gain rather than power *per se*.

Obviously, political influence can aid one in achieving economic ends, but the orientation of one who seeks power for economic ends is quite different from that of one who seeks power for its own sake. In the first case, for example, one is usually quite willing to give up power for the economic gains which one seeks. This bears, I feel, on Mills' discussion concerning the ideological shift which occurred among the small entrepreneurs as large monopolistic concerns arose. Mills sees these small entrepreneurs giving up power for 'feudal protection'.[23] Most who gave up willingly gave up because they saw economic gains for themselves in what was happening. Those who didn't see such gains fought and continue to fight.

One could go so far, in fact, as to argue that the 'political ideologies' of both the old and the new middle class are in fact anti-political in character. They are not concerned with maximizing individual political power but with maximizing individual economic gain. The capitalistic emphasis on political freedom is really an attack upon all forms of political power. The expression that the business of government is business aptly sums up this attitude.

The alienation which Marx and Mills so rightly recognize as characteristic of capitalistic societies is due not so much to the impotency of the worker, be he or she white collor or blue collar, but to the fact that in capitalistic societies political rights *per se* are seen as irrelevant. This, in part, I feel, also helps to explain why individuals in politically orientated societies, even when they themselves have little power, are often less alienated. The issue is usually not how much power do I have, but rather whether political rights, independent of economic factors, have any relevance. Mills clearly recognizes the greater importance of economic factors in American society;[24] he fails, however, fully to appreciate what this means for the political character of America.

Mills' tendency to interpret power in economic terms also serves to blind him to other, more truly political, aspects of American society. For example, while he correctly notes the non-political character of the goals of most American unions, universities, businesses and even governments, he fails to recognize the very real internal political character of these institutions. While most American institutions are more concerned with obtaining economic gains for their members than with changing the power structure of the United States, persons within these institutions are engaged in continual political battles. At times, these political battles are also in the service of economic ends; often, however, they are concerned with the actual distribution of power *per se*, i.e., the rights of individuals to control their own behaviour regardless of their economic status.

Mills' study would have benefited greatly if he had paid more attention to these non-economic political structures. He might, for example, have found that race, age and sex were important variables in these non-economic political structures. This may have allowed him to predict that the major political upheavals facing American society would grow out of the more truly political inequalities which existed. It is true that Blacks and women have been arguing for a bigger piece of the economic pie. The real thrust of these movements, as well as that of the young, has been political not economic. They want their political 'rights', that is the right to control their own actions and to have their wills respected equally. Moreover, while they see these political rights as having economic benefits, they have made it very clear that economic benefits in and of themselves will not suffice. That so many 'middle-class' white males claim not to understand what 'they' want only serves to underline the extent to which true political concerns, i.e. concerns for political rights, have historically not been a part of American political ideology.

5. The Protestant Ethic and the Spirit of Capitalism *by Max Weber*[25]

In *The Protestant Ethic and the Spirit of Capitalism*, Weber sought to support his own view regarding the multi-causal nature of social reality and more specifically the causal potential of ideas. Weber attempts to support his thesis by showing that (1) the economic conditions leading to the spirit of capitalism existed in other situations without the emergence of the spirit of capitalism and (2) that in many respects the Protestant Reformation preceded the rise of modern capitalism. The main thrust of his argument, however, is that the causal chain he hypothesizes makes more sense than the Marxist hypothesis that capitalism caused the Protestant Reformation.[26] In Weber's own terms, he attempts to support his thesis in terms of his concept of 'meaningful causality'.

Weber believed that modern capitalism required a specific orientation towards work and capital. Such an orientation, he felt could not be accounted for in purely economic terms. He argues that this orientation, which he calls the spirit of capitalism, was as much an outgrowth of another orientation, namely the Protestant ethic as vice versa. The Protestant ethic, in turn, he sees as emerging as a result of inherent contradictions in the Catholic theology of that period. More specifically, it was due to the logical contradition between the notion of an omniscient and omnipotent God and the principle that man could through his own acts affect his own destiny. He argues that one can understand the Protestant ethic as an attempt to deal with this contradiction. The Protestant resolution was to see man's destiny as predetermined. Whatever man did was according to God's will. This does not mean, however, that all men are destined to receive grace. Only those lives which are lived according to God's rules are likely to lead to eternal grace. Therefore the productive ascetic life is still seen as a sign that one is predestined for grace though it is not a means for earning grace. Though man can not earn grace, this view of the world serves to endow all works, including secular works, with a religious fervour. Each man will attempt to live his life in a manner which will indicate to himself and others that he is among the chosen. It is specifically this religious fervour, when attached to secular activities, which Weber sees as the essence of the spirit of capitalism. Secular activities acquire that character of a religious 'calling'.

In so far as Weber focuses upon the role of meaning systems to explain behaviour, it may appear that he does exactly that which I have been arguing for. To a large extent this is true. Weber probably more than any other classical theorist treats meaning systems seriously. He fails, however, to recognize fully the socio-moral character of the meaning systems he analyses. The objective of any meaning system is not only to make intellectual sense of what is happening, but to provide a basis for social solidarity, or to provide a shared 'worldview' which can hold people together.

What makes sense in one situation, however, may not make sense in another. Weber, for example, simply takes for granted the Protestant view that it makes no sense that man should be able to influence an omniscient, omnipotent God. This, however, is true only when one assumes a specific conception of omniscience and omnipotence. If one assumes that God is omniscient and omnipotent in that he knows and controls all natural sequences of events, then the Protestant view regarding man's powers over his own destiny makes sense. If omniscience means knowledge of all human intentions and omnipotence means the capability to affect all events, then the Protestant view does not necessarily hold. What is important about the Protestant ethic is not that it entailed a new conception of the relationship between God and man but that it entailed a new conception of God and the natural and social order. The Protestant ethic led not only to the rationalization of work, but to the rationalization of God and his universe. The personal, wilful God of the Old Testament has somehow been replaced by a purely cognitive Being.

In the light of points already made, I would suggest that the emergence of both the Protestant ethic and the spirit of capitalism must be explained in terms of the changing sense of meaning in Europe during the Middle Ages. This change in the sense of meaning, in turn, must be explained in terms of changes in the forms of social groups and the social importance of the intentional dimensions.

Weber and other social theorists such as Durkheim and Simmel did of course deal with these issues. It is not enough, however, to describe such changes; neither is it very useful to evolve grand theories. The intentional modality of a people, the forms of their social groupings, and their predilection for specific types of meanings are all interrelated. Each of these factors can influence the other factors in numerous ways. Any particular sequence of events is exactly that—a particular sequence of events.

This does not mean that events are not governed by general rules. It is only that the rules applicable to any given event are sufficiently numerous and complex to be unlikely to reveal themselves easily. Sociologists consequently must be ready to entertain a wide range of theoretical possibilities. Moreover, given the nature of the problem with which they are dealing—the various forms of meanings and meaning systems—they must be willing and ready to deal with moral systems in their own terms.

6. *Durkheim and Weber: Convergence or Divergence*

The prime objective of each of the studies discussed is to explain some specific social phenomenon. In an attempt to present such explanatory accounts, the authors have been forced to adopt specific theoretical orientations. In examining these studies, I have attempted to show that these orientations have built-in biases which lead the authors to see some things but to ignore others. To a large extent such bias is unavoidable. My purpose in focusing attention upon such bias has not been to eliminate theoretical bias but to indicate its existence, its consequences, and its sources. One does not eliminate a bias by recognizing it; such recognition does, however, provide the grounds for a more exhaustive account of the phenomenon in question.

When dealing with social theories rather than specific accounts, the issue is not the nature of some specific social phenomenon but the nature of social reality and social behaviour. The implications of general theoretical biases, consequently, are more ubiquitous. As a result, sociologists have an abiding interest in the convergence and divergence of different sociological schools. The general view seems to be that the more these different schools of thought converge, the greater the likelihood that they have in fact grasped the essential quality of social reality. If on the other hand they can be shown to diverge, this divergence itself must be explained.

A prime example of this type of concern is that shown towards the writings of Durkheim and Weber. Historically the major spokesman for the convergence view has been Talcott Parsons. In his book *The Structure of Social Action*, Parsons argues that Durkheim and Weber share the same basic view regarding the nature of social behaviour. Both, he maintains, hold what he calls a 'voluntaristic' view of social action, the essential elements of which entail that social behaviour be understood in terms of man's recognition and effort to conform to social norms. Parsons notes that Durkheim and Weber came to this view from very different starting points and at different times in their intellectual careers. The crucial point for Parsons, however, is that they both came to it, since such a convergence would seem to indicate the basic validity of this view.

Recently a number of social theorists have argued that Parsons' analysis is minimally misleading.[27] They have argued that Durkheim and Weber hold fundamentally different views of social behaviour. Whereas Durkheim sees social norms as controlling and constraining behaviour, Weber, they contend, emphasizes man's 'subjective' orientation and adaptation toward these norms. For Durkheim, they argue, norms govern behaviour; subjective orientation is at best secondary. For Weber, subjective orientation is of paramount importance; the meaning of any norm is determined by these subjective orientations.

While this debate may appear to be only of academic interest, it has, in fact, profound implications for the sociological enterprise itself, for it bears on the basic insight of sociology, namely, that human behaviour is often governed by normative structures and meaning systems which are part of the social world.

Durkheim and Weber were concerned with explaining human actions. Each felt that this could best be done in terms of his own view of human behaviour.

Parsons shares this concern. Like Durkheim and Weber, he is concerned with developing a theoretical perspective capable of explaining human behaviour. If he is correct—that the theoretical perspectives of Durkheim and Weber do converge—he can claim to have been successful: we will have an integrated theoretical overview, namely Parsons'. In contrast, if his critics' views are correct—and they have made a very strong case—social theorists must choose between Durkheim and Weber or some other perspective, or provide some other means for accounting for the divergence. It is not enough to say that Durkheim and Weber have different views of human behaviour. Unfortunately, I do not think Parsons is correct, although he could deal with many of the criticisms thrown at him. Durkheim and Weber do present different accounts of social action. If there is merit to both of their accounts—which is the generally accepted view—how is this possible? The answer, I feel, has already been presented. Durkheim and Weber, for the most part, utilize different sociological approaches. More specifically, Durkheim employs primarily a socio-cultural approach whereas Weber employs a social class approach.[28]

Given Durkheim's concern with the division of labour, his analyses of various social strata and Weber's concern for various religious ideologies and cultural groups, such an assertion may initially appear fallacious if not ludicrous. There is a fundamental difference, however, between the concepts that a sociologist may use and his basic approach. Durkheim is primarily concerned with the problem of social solidarity; Weber's primary concern is meaningful social action. This difference leads Durkheim and Weber to focus their attentions not only upon different aspects of meaning systems but upon different types of meaning systems.

Durkheim argues that social solidarity, whatever form it later takes, is initially due to 'mechanical causes'. 'What brings men together are mechanical causes and impulsive forces, such as affinity of blood, attachment to the same soil, ancestral worship, community of habits, etc. It is only when the group has been formed on these bases that cooperation is organized there.'[29] In short, the meaning systems or moral orders that Durkheim sees as giving birth to societies are generated by men in so far as they constitute a people. It is true that Durkheim himself defines mechanical solidarity in terms of similarity which would seem to reflect what has been defined as the social class approach. The similarities that Durkheim focuses upon, however, are not similarities due to the distribution of social resources, but similarities due to physical conditions. Among these physical conditions, shared territory is the most important. Such meaning systems exhibit the constraining character that Durkheim attributes to them.

This does not mean that Durkheim does not recognize the importance of 'subjective' self-interest. Parsons is correct in arguing that he does. Such an orientation becomes important for Durkheim, however, only in societies characterized by a high degree of division of labour. The reason for this is that in such societies social solidarity is based upon a different type of moral order, namely one based upon cooperation. Parsons' critics are correct, however, in arguing that for Durkheim the former type of moral order remains dominant at least in so far as Durkheim's general view of society is concerned. For Durkheim the moral order is basically an external constraining force.

Weber, in contrast, as noted above, is primarily concerned with meaningful social action, i.e. social action dependent upon the interests of actors. This leads Weber to focus his attention upon different types of meaning systems from those analysed by Durkheim. Weber himself is clearly aware of this. In defining social action he presents four basic types:

Social action, like other forms of action, may be classified in the following four types according to its mode of orientation: (1) in terms of rational orientation to a system of discrete individual ends (zweckrational), that is, through expectations as to the behaviour of objects in the external situation and of other human individuals, making use of these expectations as 'conditions' or 'means' for the successful attainment of the actor's own rationally chosen ends; (2) in terms of rational orientation to an absolute value (wertrational); involving a conscious belief in the absolute value of some ethical, aesthetic, religious, or other form of behaviour, entirely for its own sake and independently of any prospect of external success; (3) in terms of affectual orientation, especially emotional, determined by the specific affects and states of feeling of the actor; (4) traditionally oriented, through the habituation of long practice.[30]

Of these four, three have some affinity with Durkheim's view of mechanical solidarity and hence his general view about the relationship between social behaviour and the normative structures: the absolute value orientation, the affectual orientation and the traditional orientation. It is, however, the means-end rational orientation which is of central importance in Weber's political and economic writings and best typifies to Weber our common-sense notion of 'rational action'. He goes so far, in fact, as to label affectual and traditional orientations as 'borderline' types of social action; he similarly refers to the 'irrational' aspect of value rationality when it is pushed to its extremes. This is not surprising since it is the means-end rational orientation which most relies upon the self-interest of actors which is clearly Weber's main concern.

While Parsons is correct in arguing that there is a good deal of overlap between Durkheim's and Weber's general views of social behaviour, his critics are also correct in arguing that the two men held fundamentally different views on social behaviour. This was because they were interested in different problems.

Was Weber, however, interested in means-end rational orientations only because they better serve self-interest, or was there something else which led him not only to means-end rational orientations but also to his concern with 'interest'? As indicated above, I think his general concern with class structure and economic interest groups was important to him. As noted earlier social classes and interest groups generate their own ideational structures. Since the existence of one interest group generally entails the existence of other, often conflicting interest groups, each interest group must normally take into consideration the interests of other groups. As such, these ideational structures do have an integrating function; this is not, however, their primary function as is the case with Durkheim's moral orders.

It may be argued that a concern for meaning systems which stress means-ends rationality would mesh better with a social system approach than a social class approach. This is true only when the ends are given clear priority over the means, which, in turn, requires a high degree of consensus regarding these ends. Such a consensus would serve, however, to undermine the importance of the self-interest of the actors. It was specifically these self interests which were of major concern to Weber, hence his concern with interest groups over social systems *per se* (or alternatively, given Weber's interest in interest groups, hence his concern with self interest orientations).

In this regard, it might be noted that a social system approach, in so far as it stresses ends over means, manages to integrate both the constraining aspects of the socio-cultural approach and the self-interest orientations emphasis of the social class approach, though in doing so it also blunts the impact of both. In the light of this fact, it is not surprising to find that Parsons himself utilizes primarily a social system approach.

I have here only touched on a very complex theoretical issue. However, perhaps enough evidence has been presented to support the major thesis that the debate over the convergence or divergence of Durkheim and Weber results from a failure to recognize that they utilize fundamentally different sociological approaches which emphasize different types of meaning systems and different types of social behaviour.

7. The Sociological Dilemma

While the question of whether Weber's and Durkheim's views converge or diverge has contemporary theoretical applicability, it is primarily a question of historical significance. There is another question related to the general issue of the nature of meaning systems which is, for all practical purposes, a new one. I refer to what may be called the ethnomethodological question which I would formulate as follows: What is the relationship between the 'rules of action' used in explaining behaviour and such explanations themselves?

Initially the answer to this question may appear to be self-evident. Such 'rules of action' provide the bases for such explanations. Such an answer would seem to be consistent with everything said above. Sociologists seek to explain behaviour by discovering the various rules of action which govern these behaviours. There is, however, a catch to such an answer. Its source is to be found in our very account of such rules of action.

What is the function of rules of action and the meaning systems from which they are derived? To help man make his world a more ordered world with all of its supposedly beneficial results. What is the relationship between such rules of action and sociology itself? Clearly, sociology as a discipline not only studies various rules of action but entails its own rules of action otherwise known as the sociological criteria. This raises an interesting possibility, namely, that the rules of action and the meaning systems which sociologists 'discover' are as much a product of sociologists' need to order their world as they are the product of the needs of the persons studied to order their world. To put this a slightly different way, sociological explanations may be determined, as much if not more, by sociologists' need to explain as by the so-called real world which is to be explained.

The issue of sociological bias is, of course, not new. The fact that social theorists may interpret events to serve their own needs has been recognized for centuries. For the most part, however, such criticisms were aimed at the personal biases of a particular theorist. This is not to say that the problem of systematic, theoretical bias has not received its share of criticism. Weber, for one, deals with it directly in presenting his concept of *verstehen*. He states quite clearly that the sociologist, if he hopes to explain what is going on, must attempt to see the world through the eyes of those he is studying if an adequate account is to be had. It can be argued, in fact, that he confronted the ethnomethodological question before there were any ethnomethodologists.

The ethnomethodologists, however, raise questions that go beyond Weber's analysis. Weber recognized the need to take into account the motivational factors governing social behaviour. He argues that we can understand social action only if we can put ourselves in the place of those studied. Weber differs from modern ethnomethodologists, however, in his belief that this can always be done. He believes this because he assumes that only specific types of rationality underlie all social action. In short, by assuming certain patterns of thought to be universal, Weber believes that we can put ourselves in the place of those whom we study.

It is specifically these patterns of rational thought that the ethnomethodologist questions. The form of this questioning, however, differs from one methodologist to another. Some argue that such patterns simply do not exist; others argue that we don't know if they exist or not; yet others believe that they do exist but that we still don't know what they are.[31] Each of these views has given rise to its own forms of sociological investigations. Those who believe that it is impossible to grasp the rationalities of those studied, tend to emphasize the dramatic character of sociological accounts. Those who believe that it is possible to grasp these rationalities, tend to focus upon everyday activities and the rationalities of common sense. Those engaged in these latter pursuits have also developed an interest in phenomenological investigations. Those who don't know whether such rationalities can be grasped or not mix these concerns. All, however, tend to reject grand theorizing; they reject it because they believe that grand theorizing requires that we understand the rationalities of social behaviour and this, they believe, is not yet, if it is ever to be, the case.

Studies of everyday activities, phenomenological-like investigations, and critiques of grand theories are all useful. Each of these approaches, however, tends to circumvent, if not avoid, the main issue by focusing upon the rationalities of specific behaviours or specific orientations rather than the rationality of meaning systems *per se*. The primary concern of sociology is not how men interact nor how man as an individual thinks, but rather how men as members of social groups order their world. Individual behaviour and individual attitudes are important, but only in so far as they can be placed within a sociological context.

How, it might be asked, are we to place man within a sociological context if we don't know the nature of this context;

how can we explain, or even describe, such behaviour and attitudes in terms of the rationality of a governing meaning system if we don't understand the rationality of the meaning system? Wouldn't all such efforts, as some ethnomethodologists suggest, be futile at best? Yes, if one simply accepts a given rationality as the rationality of the meaning system under investigation. No, if one is able to examine the rationality of a given meaning system in terms of the range of possible rationalities.

The question is, however, how can such a range of possible rationalities be determined? The answer, I feel, rests upon the fact that sociologists and social theorists are members of their own societies. Any social theory, consequently, can be seen not only as an effort to make sense out of the rationality of a given society, but also as influenced by the rationality of the society from which it emerges.

The point made here is similar to the guiding principle of the sociology of knowledge approach, namely, that the way man sees the world is influenced, if not determined, by his social position. The principle is here applied to sociologists themselves, however, rather than to some other group. There is another difference. The sociology of knowledge approach attempts primarily to understand the inherent biases of particular worldviews in terms of the social conditions which gave rise to that particular worldview. To do this, of course, requires that we understand the rationality of the social world under investigation which, in turn, puts us back where we began. The argument is not that we attempt to discover the biases of particular social theories, but rather that we focus upon the rationality of the social theory itself. While this is often difficult, it is considerably easier than trying to discover the rationalities inherent in the unformulated world views of everyday life. By focusing upon a wide range of such theories, we can begin to map out the range of possible rationalities.[32]

Admittedly, 'new' theories can emerge at any time. I would suggest, however, that most such 'new' theories would prove upon analysis to contain essentially the same elements as are in older theories. The mix might be different, but the components would not be. In this way, we should be able at least to begin to unravel the various elements that go into any meaning system. This is, of course, basically what both the ethnomethodologist and the phenomenologist claim to be doing. What is being suggested here, however, is that both the ethnomethodologist and the phenomenologist are directing their attentions to the wrong, or at least less rewarding, places. If we are concerned with the rationalities of socially generated meaning systems, then we must examine such meaning systems. Neither specific rules of action applicable to specific situations nor the structure of individual minds constitute such meaning systems. In contrast sociological and other social scientific theories, as well as religious ideologies, myths, etc., do provide data for discovering such rationalities.

D. SOME FINAL COMMENTS ON THE NATURE OF SOCIOLOGY

This study is subtitled an essay in philosophical sociology because it aptly conforms to Simmel's conception of such a study, namely, one that is concerned with '. . . the conditions, fundamental concepts, and presuppositions of concrete research . . . (and the) . . . completions, connections, questions and concepts that have no place in experience and in immediately objective knowledge.'[33] In light of the above it might now appear as if I am arguing that philosophical sociology should become one, if not the, major concern of sociology *per se*.

To a large extent this is the case. There is, however, one major difference, namely, that I believe that the underlying concepts of sociology do have a place in experience though they are seldom present in a highly visible form; or, to put it more accurately, I believe the underlying concepts of sociology and the underlying concepts of everyday life share a common origin, namely, the categories of social experience. This is not a unique position. It is, I would argue, the view of Durkheim, Weber, and Mead; it also has much in common with the structural views of Claude Levi-Strauss and the developmental theories of Jean Piaget. It is, however, not a very popular sociological view.

This might seem surprising in the light of the centrality of meaning systems for sociology. Sociologists, however, have tended to separate mind and the external social world. To a large extent this has been due to their desire to be 'scientific', to deal with an 'external empirical reality' on the one hand and individual minds on the other. In part, I think it has also been due to a desire to avoid many of the philosophical paradoxes that have traditionally been associated with the nature of knowledge. Unfortunately, the baby has been thrown out with the bathwater, since any account of knowledge must eventually deal with mind.

This is not to deny that it is possible to study sociology without getting involved with 'philosophical' issues, providing that one's concerns are fairly concrete. These issues cannot be avoided, however, when one attempts more general theoretical syntheses; to deal with forms of knowledge and meaning systems in a pure way, it is necessary to deal with general categories of mind.

Categories of mind are not the subject matter of theoretical sociology. The subject matter of sociology remains social behaviour, social groups and meaning systems: categories of mind in and of themselves can explain none of these things. On the other hand, none of these things can be explained without taking into consideration the categories of mind. We might say that they are built into the data of sociology. This is, of course, the case with nearly all of the social sciences. Sociology is distinct, however, in that its concern with meaning systems provides an arena for studying the entire range of such categories and rules of mind unequalled by the other social sciences. For better or worse, the reverse relationship also holds; of all the social sciences, sociology must deal with the greatest range of such categories and rules of mind.

Two final points. The view of social reality entailed by this neo-Kantian orientation neither allows for a purely deductive sociology nor necessitates a relativistic one. Categories of mind, no matter how important they might be, cannot in and of themselves account for any meaning system. Concrete meaning systems are generated by specific patterns of social contact and must be treated as the empirical items that they are.

This does not mean that all meaning systems are equally 'valid'. Different meaning systems do not satisfy equally even their own criteria. Admittedly, these criteria differ. A meaning system which may be valid by one set of criteria may not be valid by another. Such a situation can create difficulties. Can a sociologist, for example, tell if a particular meaning system works in a particular situation or can he even judge why it exists? The answer to both questions is yes. It is up to the sociologist, however, to prove his case within the context that he works.

IV
Summary and Concluding Comments

This study has attempted to reveal the underlying conceptual structure upon which sociology rests. It has focused specifically on the following issues: (1) the social sciences and the Intentional Frame of Reference; (2) meaning systems and their relationship to sociology; (3) various forms of social contact and their bearing on the dominant sociological approaches; (4) the use of non-normative groups in sociological theorizing and the intermeshing of theoretically distinct sociological approaches; and (5) the theoretical implications of sociology's reliance upon meaning systems to explain social behaviour.

As indicated towards the end of the last chapter, if sociology is ever to come to grips with its own basic vision of society, it must, among other things, re-examine itself in terms of its own vision. It is clearly beyond the scope of this book to do so in any exhaustive manner. Nevertheless, by way of a concluding example that may help to synthesize much of what has been said, I should like to suggest the form that such a sociology of sociology might take.

Sociology as a particular meaning system can be approached in various ways. It can be analysed primarily in socio-cultural terms, social class/interest group terms, or social system/social network terms. Though there is a significant amount of overlap, each approach has its own distinctive character.

A. A SOCIOLOGY OF SOCIOLOGY—ANOTHER VIEW

1. Sociology as a Cultural Phenomenon

To conceive of sociology as a cultural phenomenon is to see it as part of the general meaning system which we all hold. It is a system of values, meaning and beliefs which we use to order and explain our world. As such it may be considered as a type of religious faith. There is still the question of why this particular 'faith' evolved when and where it did. What was the character of our forefathers which made it susceptible to the sociological worldview? While no definitive answer is possible, certain factors appear to be relevant.

The prime function of any culture, as noted earlier, is to provide a sense of order capable of preserving social solidarity. Cultures attempt to 'justify' the existence of a people as a people. As they and the social bonds that hold them together change, so must their culture. New forms of social relationships and new peoples must be accounted for. Any meaning system, however, has only so much flexibility; it can tolerate only so much strain before it must give way to a new view capable of making sense of the new reality. The sociological perspective can be seen as such a new view. It provides a means for making sense of complex, heterogeneous men and women, and provides the ideological grounds for the social solidarity of such people. It does all this by providing a 'new way' of looking at man, whereby each new social relationship does not strain our conception of man, but rather supplements it. A way where each new form of social relationship does not undermine our sense of social solidarity but rather strengthens it.

This thesis is well stated in Russell Dynes's article 'Sociology as a Religious Movement.'[1] He notes that Raymond Aron suggests that sociology can be seen as reflecting the 'consciousness' of modern society. He notes that it was not only Comte who saw sociology as a new religion but also that the works of Marx, Durkheim and Weber had a religious tone. Nearly all new perspectives are introduced with religious fervour. Sociology was unique in that it not only provided a new theology, but a theology capable of explaining the complexities of modern societies.

2. Sociology as Class Ideology

The view that sociology reflects class biases has much in common with the view that sociology is a cultural product. In both cases sociology is seen as having a definite social function. The social class view differs from the cultural view in that, rather than emphasizing the ordering and solidarity functions of sociology, it emphasizes specific class interests. It can be seen as serving the interests of those seeking social change. It does this by revealing the relative character of all social orders. It allows people to see how specific social orders serve the interests of various groups. This knowledge can enhance class consciousness.

Sociology can also be used by those seeking to maintain the *status quo*. By emphasizing the complexity of social structures, one can argue that radical change is likely to generate all sorts of unanticipated detrimental consequences. What is important from our point of view is not the specific class bias, i.e., whether sociology is used to support or stifle change, but the fact that sociology can be seen as a product of class conflict.

One can argue, of course, that class conflict is characteristic of nearly all societies, but that sociology has arisen only recently. Here is would be necessary to note the complex character of modern societies and their class structures. This admittedly appears to put sociology more into a cultural context than a class context. There is, however, an important difference. Sociology is not seen as a means of dealing with social complexity *per se* as in the cultural view, but with the intricacies of specific class positions.

The class view of sociology has both advantages and disadvantages compared to the cultural view. On the positive side it can explain different 'sociologies'; different classes are obviously likely to generate different views of society. On the negative side, this very diversity makes it difficult if not impossible to obtain a 'true' view. This problem was clearly recognized by Karl Mannheim, who in effect held a class view of the origin of sociology.[2] For Mannheim the resolution was for sociologists to establish themselves as a distinct interest group. Given their marginal status, a point noted earlier by Simmel, Mannheim saw this as a real possibility. Sociologists must free themselves from their own class biases; they should become 'sociologist kings'. For Mannheim, however, all knowledge including sociology is inherently ideological (class orientated).

3. Sociology: A Product of the Division of Labour

The system/network approach would see sociology primarily as a product of the division of labour within academic institutions. Sociology is neither a religion nor a class ideology. It is a specific orientation peculiar to specific individuals who occupy specific institutional roles. It evolved as these roles evolved. What is distinctive about sociology is not so much its view of the world, but the fact that specific individuals, sociologists, have accepted it as their view. This is not to deny that there is something distinctive about this orientation in and of itself. There is. The orientation, however, did not give rise to sociology; sociology gave rise to the orientation. Sociology, in turn, did not produce sociologists; sociologists gave rise to sociology. Sociologists, in turn, did not organize departments of sociology; departments of sociology produced sociologists. Departments of sociology exist in turn because academic institutions have evolved in accordance with the division of labour. Sociology, in short, is merely one discipline among many, each of which is the result of years of greater and greater intellectual specialization (division of labour). [3]

If one wishes to understand sociology as it is today, one must retrace the history of intellectual specialization. One must begin with Greek philosophy and trace its evolution into the distinctive schools of theology, humanities and sciences. The emergence of the social sciences must be mapped. The growth of various departments of social psychology, the split between departments of anthropology/sociology, etc. all must be analysed. One must similarly examine the new alliances which emerged as the process of specialization unfolded. [4] Furthermore, one must not limit oneself to the 'history of ideas'. Political, economic and social factors must also be taken into account. New disciplines and departments have often been due as much to personal conflicts between men as they have to theoretical differences. To quote Everett Hughes, 'Sociology is what sociologists do.' [5] To understand sociology, therefore, it is necessary to understand sociology as a profession.

While the socio-cultural, class, and social system approaches present us with their own versions of the growth of sociology, they agree that sociology emerged during a crucial period in the history of western civilization. They all see sociology as one of the outgrowths of the increased complexities of western civilization. We might say that they see sociology as a discipline born with the emergence of new, distinct, yet overlapping, social groupings.

As such, the birth of sociology did not just entail a new way of looking at social reality; in a very real sense, it reflected a new social reality itself. This new world which sociology saw was itself the father of sociology. Sociology not only sensitized man to the problems of social order, but the emerging problems of social order gave birth to sociology.

Conflicting and competing world views, of course, existed before there was a discipline of sociology. Each of these worldviews existed primarily in isolation from other worldviews, however, so that people were relatively protected from exposure to conflicting ideologies. In such a situation, people tend to develop an immunity towards doubt; their truth is the only truth. With increased exposure to other worldviews, this immunity to doubt is destroyed. New ways for coping with conflicting ideologies are required; sociology represented one such way.

There is still the question, of course, as to why the old social orders gave way. Why did new social groupings emerge? Why did previously isolated peoples begin to interact? Why did people begin to see themselves differently? This is perhaps the sociological $64.00 question. It is a question with which Spencer, Comte, Durkheim, Marx, Weber, and Simmel all wrestled. Where Spencer saw it as merely another instance of the general evolutionary process whereby the simple becomes more complex, Comte saw in it a more specifically sociological process reflecting various stages of civilization. Durkheim stressed the impact of population growth and the resultant increase in types of social contacts. Marx emphasized man's longing for control over and freedom from his environment, and the resultant technological innovations which in turn necessitated social changes. Weber, while recognizing the impact of political and economic factors, stressed the importance of changing value systems themselves, whereas Simmel focused his attention upon the actual form of social association.

None of these views have won out over the others. The basic question remains unanswered and sociologists continue to confront it. What is clear is that the emergence of sociology must not only be understood in an historical context, but in a sociologically enlightened historical context. This requires (1) examining historical facts in terms of the social orders which pertained during the periods under investigation, and (2) examining these orders in terms of the social groupings which existed at the time. It will also require that sociologists possess a philosophical-theological sensitivity towards moral orders which they have by and large rejected as irrelevant to their professional concerns.

B. FINAL WORD

In concluding, I should like to re-emphasize that for sociologists to deal with moral systems in their own terms it is necessary for them to possess a philosophical-theological sensitivity which they have largely rejected as irrelevant to their professional concerns. This does not mean that sociologists should become philosophers or theologians. As Durkheim rightly noted, sociology is the *scientific study* of ethics. The sociologist is not concerned with the realm of moral possibilities in and of themselves; he is concerned with actual moral orders. He cannot hope to make sense of these actual moral orders, however, unless he has some awareness of what the various possibilities are. This means that he must confront various questions which have traditionally been the property of philosophers and theologians. Classical philosophical questions such as the relationship of the one and the many, free will and determinism, oughts and cans, and the concepts of negation, similarity, implications, etc. are inherent to any meaning system. If we are to explain human behaviour in terms of meaning systems, we must be capable of dealing with these meaning systems.

I personally believe that sociology has something very important to say about the nature of human behaviour. In order for it to fulfil its own destiny, however, it must be true to its own vision. Sociologists must cease serving false gods. Sociology has profited greatly from the insights of the physical sciences and the other social sciences. None of these disciplines, however, see man as the moral being that sociology does. Only by accepting man as a moral being and by treating moral orders in their own terms can sociologists hope to add to our understanding of man. If they do accept this challenge, they will not only generate useful sociological insights but also contribute to the broader philosophical goals of indicating the significance of sociology for the 'totality of mind, life and being in general'. [6]

It should be noted that for those who attempt to follow this path, there are costs. Professionals in any field do not take lightly having their most cherished beliefs scrutinized. This is a fact which every sociologist should recognize. When such beliefs are subject to scrutiny without any immediate payoff, the costs can become quite high. It would be lovely if I could give assurance that such efforts will always bear fruit. Such, however, is not the case. Philosophical inquiry raises more questions than it answers; one's answers furthermore are always open to supplementary revision if not rejection. There is also, however, the excitement and joy of engaging in a most meaningful intellectual pursuit.

Notes

PART I: THE INTENTIONALITY AND MODALITY
OF SOCIAL BEHAVIOUR

[1] For an excellent discussion of the relationship of 'objectivity' and science, see Israel Scheffler, *Science and Subjectivity* (Indianapolis, New York, Kansas City: Bobbs-Merrill, 1967).

[2] These criteria have been embodied in various philosophic schools. The empirical criteria is most often associated with British Empiricism and later Logical Positivism; the rational criteria is most often associated with Continental Reationalism. See *Our Philosophical Traditions*, by Sterling P. Lamprecht (New York: Appleton-Century Croft, 1955). I might add that revelation has also been claimed as a means to 'truth', but few have claimed for revelation an 'objective' status.

[3] The summary of Kant presented is based upon a wide variety of sources, including oral comments. It is primarily based, however, upon my own reading and interpretation of Kant's *Critique of Pure Reason*, trans. Norman Kemp-Smith (London: Macmillan & Co., 1958). For a highly regarded treatment of the problem of perspective as it relates to scientific knowledge, see Thomas Kuhn's *The Structure of Scientific Revolution* (Chicago: Chicago University Press, 1962/1970).

[4] David Hume, *An Essay Concerning Human Understanding*.

[5] For an outline of the various philosophic schools of the period, see Sterling P. Lamprecht, *Our Philosophical Traditions* (New York: Appleton-Century-Croft, 1955).

[6] Categories of experience are distinguished from categories of understanding in that they govern the manner in which we can experience the external world in contrast to the manner in which we can conceptually organize these experiences. Kant's point is that any knowledge which claims to be based upon empirical experience must be grounded upon such categories of experience, that is, one's

categories of understanding must be consistent with categories of experience.

[7] In addition to Scheffler, *op. cit.*, see C. I. Lewis, *Mind and the World Order* (New York: Dover, 1956); W. Quine, *Word and Object* (New York: Wiley, 1960); and P. Strawson, *Individuals* (London: Methuen, 1959). These authors differ on various points, but there is general agreement on the main issue referred to in the text.

[8] The term 'ideational' is used here and throughout the text as the generic term to include ideas, values, beliefs, meanings, norms, etc. My usage is similar to that of Sorokin's.

[9] The term 'simpler' is used here solely in reference to the relative role of ideational factors in these various disciplines.

[10] The term 'intentional' is used here and throughout the text in the same or similar sense as that in which it is used by Hampshire (1959), rather than in the sense of the phenomenologists, who follow Husserl's use of the term. As such, all knowledge is regarded as the result of an active mind, but this mind is not restricted to pure *a priori* data. It rather accepts the view that this mind is in contact with a real, external world. One is still concerned with the *a priori* properties of mind, but mind *per se* is seen as possible only in its relationship to a world beyond it. In this regard the position being presented is similar to the views of conceptual pragmatism.

[11] The statements in the text pertaining to maturation and cognitive development are drawn primarily from the works of Piaget, Sullivan and Erikson. (See bibliography.) For a general outline, see John H. Flavell, *The Developmental Psychology of Jean Piaget* (Princeton: D. Van Nostrand, 1963).

[12] The concept of power as used here and throughout the text refers primarily to the ability to govern action as a direct result of what one wills. As such, the power of any individual is determined by the 'zone of jurisdiction' of his will. So defined, my concept of power is very similar to that of Erikson and Piaget. It differs from Weber's view (*The Theory of Social and Economic Organization*, p. 152), in that it does not assume the need for resistance. In defining power in terms of one's ability to overcome resistance, Weber limits the relevancy of power to those situations where there is a conflict of wills. It is true that a person's power is often defined in terms of his power compared to that of another person; this, however, is not always the case. The fact that I do not have the power to fly has nothing to do with the relative powers of other persons.

[13] In psychoanalytic literature, the concern with power as an

analytically separate concern from gratification *per se*, is perhaps most clearly reflected in Alfred Adler's modifications of classical Freudian theory. See Alfred Adler, *The Individual Psychology of Alfred Adler*, ed. and annotated by Henry L. and Rowene R. Ansbacher (New York: Modern Library, 1944).

[14] In the light of points made earlier, it should be clear that I do not believe that there is any such thing as purely non-cognitive experience; there is no pure given in human experience. I use the term 'raw' experience to describe those experiences which are structured only in terms of the *a priori* categories of naive experience.

[15] I refer here to conceptual pragmatists such as Lewis, *op. cit.*, C. Peirce, and John Dewey. (See bibliography.) Among more recent philosophers who have dealt with this problem, see Stuart Hampshire and his *Thought and Action* (London: Chatto and Windus, 1959). For a popular rendition of Whitehead's views, see his *Science and the Modern World* (New York: Macmillan, 1925); for a more systematic presentation, see his *Process and Reality* (New York: Macmillan, 1929). For Bergson, see Henri Bergson, *Creative Evolution* (New York: Modern Library, 1944).

[16] It is only fair to note, however, that I feel that such is the case. Here I would again recommend the works of Whitehead, Peirce, Lewis, and Bergson.

[17] It is somewhat misleading to talk about 'strict behaviourists' today since few behaviourists still conform to Watson's rigid principles. His basic vision, however, still pervades the works of most modern behaviourists including that of Skinner. For an excellent review of behaviourism, or as it is today also labelled Stimulus-Response theory, see Berger and Lambert, 'Stimulus-Response Theory in Contemporary Social Psychology' in *The Handbook of Social Psychology*, ed. Lindzey and Aronson (Reading, Mass.: Addison-Wesley, 1968), vol. 1, pp. 81–178.

The behaviourist's black box view is basically as follows: Human behaviour may be influenced by the way men experience their world. It is impossible, however, to treat such experiences scientifically; they are not amenable to objective study. It is possible, however, to study objectively the conditions which give rise to specific behaviours. All scientific talk of 'experience', in fact, must itself be reducible to observable behaviour.

To give an example: To explain why X strikes Y, it is necessary to know the conditions which stimulated X so to behave. X may say that he did it because Y made him angry, but to the strict behaviourist this tells us nothing. We must know what Y did to bring on X's violence. To talk of anger as the cause of X's act is, according to the strict behaviourist, to engage in a form of sophistry. We can talk scientifically of 'anger' only in behavioural terms; the act of striking Y can be called an angry act. In short, according to the strict behaviourist, the social scientist must limit himself to objectively observable data as he considers the physical scientist does.

While the behaviourist's credo may appear to satisfy the criteria of objectivity (as he interprets it) or the physical sciences, it necessitates a fundamental philosophical revision. The behaviourist may claim to be uninterested in what happens in the black box, but he is nevertheless stuck with it. The way man experiences his world may not be 'scientifically' relevant, but the fact that man experiences his world, whether the behaviourist likes it or not, is part of his 'philosophic' worldview. The behaviourist himself may be able to ignore such experiences (though I should add I have found few who do so consistently), but a philosophical analysis of the behaviourist's perspective cannot. In other words, while a behaviourist may claim to be uninterested in what goes on in his black box, a philosophic analysis of the behaviourist's orientation cannot ignore it.

This analysis of behaviourism may strike many behaviourists as misleading if not simply wrong. These behaviourists would argue that they do not deal with human experiences in any form. Some would even argue that they do not deal with what might be called experiential dimensions such as pain and pleasure. Here I can only argue that the analysis presented is, in my opinion, an accurate account of the underlying conceptual system used by the behaviourist. Fortunately, however, this difference of opinion, given the objectives of this book, need not overly concern us. If a behaviourist wants to claim that he or she does not deal with human experiences in any way and that what is presented as the behaviourist's view is really at best a neobehaviourist view, he or she may do so, since I am primarily concerned with describing the step by step modifications of the object frame of reference required by sociology. If the modifications attributed to behaviourism are more accurately attributed to neo-behaviourists, it doesn't really matter. What does matter is that such modificiations must be introduced somewhere if we are to treat human experiences as relevant to an account of human behaviour. If a behaviourist rejects such experiences as relevant, he or she is simply left with an even more limited view of human behaviour than that presented in the text.

It may be argued that philosophically the physical scientists are confronted with a similar dilemma. They must also assume that for A to cause B to respond in some way, B must in some way 'apperceive', to use Whitehead's term, A. The behaviourist's dilemma is somewhat more complex, however, in that he is forced to assert properties which the physical scientists need not assert. He may choose not to talk about the experiences of pain and pleasure, but he cannot avoid talking about pain and pleasure stimuli or, at least, approach/avoidance behaviour.

To assert that a pain/pleasure or approach/avoidance dimension is necessary to explain human behaviour makes eminently good common sense. People appear to seek pleasure and to avoid pain. Such, in fact, appears to be one, if not the primary, rule of human behaviour. Human beings initially rely almost completely upon this pain/pleasure or gratification dimension in defining the world about them. A newborn infant might be able to distinguish colours, smells, forms, etc., but all such characteristics play a secondary role to that of pleasure and pain. It is in terms of pleasure and pain that the world is defined. Mother may be tall, short, fat, thin, white skinned, black skinned, etc.; it really doesn't matter. What is important is the fact that she is an object of pleasure. The same can be said of various types of food and other inanimate objects. Similarly, what is important about a dirty diaper, a cold bath, etc., is not the fact that it has a certain smell, a certain colour, a certain texture, etc., but the fact that it is non-pleasurable.

It may be argued that it is specifically certain combinations of smells, colours, textures, tastes, temperatures, etc. which the child finds pleasurable and non-pleasurable. Such, however, does not seem to be the case. It is only later that the child learns to associate these more specific sensory characteristics to the previously labelled pleasurable and non-pleasurable objects. In short, pleasure and pain depend upon something apart from these sensory characteristics. It is specifically this difference which has to modify the object frame of reference, as defined by Kant. It requires such a modification, because neither pain nor pleasure can be considered 'real' in Kant's object frame of reference.

Pain and pleasure could be defined in terms of specific behavioural responses which could, in turn, be described as empirical 'givens', but even if this were done, one wouldn't get back to the object frame of reference. The world would have been redefined since the behaviour in question would still be seen as having been caused by factors which themselves are not describable in terms of properties that belong to the object frame of reference.

It is not that one can't deal with pain and pleasure 'empirically', but just that in Kant's object frame of reference, such dimensions don't pertain to 'objects'.

It may be argued that one can describe even the stimulus in purely 'physical' terms, i.e., heat, conductivity, etc. One could say, for example, that a person will remove his or her hand from an object with a temperature of over 180°F. and thereby avoid any mention of pain. To do this is to engage in sophistry, however, since it is not the heat which is seen as causing the behaviour but the pain. I would argue, in fact, that even the strictest of behaviourists would have to admit that at one level he or she sees human behaviour as determined, in some way, by human experiences, which are describable only in terms of non-physical dimensions.

[18] I might just note here that there are times when we do use a notion of physical behaviour in understanding human behaviour. If, for example, we observed a large man knock over a small woman in a rush to get somewhere, our understanding of what happened, i.e., the woman being knocked down, would be based upon knowledge of the rules governing matter in motion.

[19] The following summary of Mead is based primarily upon his *Mind, Self and Society* (Chicago: University of Chicago Press, 1934).

[20] For a discussion dealing with the difference between recognized meaning and meaning *per se*, see pp. 12–13.

[21] There are few examples of a person making the jump from signs to symbols as dramatic as that of Helen Keller in *The Miracle Worker*. Near the end of the play we see this blind, deaf, but highly intelligent girl suddenly realize that the taps on her hand which previously called out in her the responses of 'drinking', 'being washed', 'running to avoid rain', etc. is in fact the name for water which she can contemplate without response.

It is interesting to note that Mead's analysis would seem to explain the fairly recent findings and theories (rejected by Wilson in his *Sociobiology*, pp. 473–478), regarding dolphins, namely, that dolphins may also have the ability to think meaningfully. Dolphins, like man, have a large brain for their body size, are social, and also rely heavily upon verbal or, more accurately, auditory signs. According to Mead's analysis, in fact, the probabilities would be that dolphins do engage in meaningful communication.

[22] Wittgenstein, from a very different beginning, reaches relatively the same conclusion regarding the social character of all meanings. See his *Philosophical Investigations* (New York: Macmillan, 1953), especially I, pp. 198–293. See also Peter Winch,

The Idea of a Social Science (London: Routledge and Kegan Paul, 1958), pp. 24–39.

[23] This same point was emphasized by Max Weber who came to it from a very different direction. It is embodied in his concept of *verstehen*. More recently, it has received considerable attention from Winch (1958), Louch (1966) and various 'ethnomethodologists', who give credit not only to Weber, but also to Wittgenstein, *op. cit.* For two excellent, recent reviews of these developments, see Bernstein (1976) and Giddens.

[24] Mead does not actually discuss either a gratification or a power dimension. He implicitly makes use of these dimensions, but he does not explicitly say so.

[25] It might be noted that all behaviourists, even those who claim not to deal with human experiences, engage in this sort of analysis. The behaviourist himself consequently deals with meanings in Mead's sense of the term even if he denies the existence of meaningful behaviour to those he studies.

[26] In light of Mead's analysis, one could argue that all dimensions, including those directly experienced by our senses, are 'intentional/subjective' in so far as they are based on the way we respond to particular stimuli. Nevertheless the quality 'red' appears to most people to be more 'real', more 'objective' than do the intentional dimensions. It may be true that our experience of redness may be based in part upon how we as human beings respond to a specific external stimulus, but there remains a feeling that such dimensions are less dependent upon man and more dependent upon what is out there than such qualities as 'pleasurable' or 'powerful'. In a sense this is true; there is a difference. This difference, however, is merely a difference of time.

All responses require time. All conscious perceptions, therefore, require time. To be able to say that something is red, for example, requires that sufficient time elapse to allow us to respond to the given stimulus. Certain dimensions, however, require less time than do others. As a result, certain dimensions can be tested more quickly than can others. If I hand you an object and say 'this is heavy', you can determine if in fact it is heavy, i.e., if the pressure in your hand corresponds to the pressure you would expect from a heavy object, almost immediately. Other dimensions require more time to be verified. If I say, for example, that the roast chicken is delicious, you must take a bite, chew it, savour it and swallow it before you would be in a position to agree or disagree.

The main thing that distinguishes the intentional dimensions from sensory dimensions is that the intentional dimensions require more time for response. This is due to the fact that the responses required to justify assigning such dimensions are dependent upon events which themselves take more time to unfold. As a result, we are more aware of the response element. This, in turn, leads us to believe that such dimensions depend more upon our responses than upon what is supposedly out there. This is generally not the case, however; it is only that it takes longer for what is out there to reveal itself. Admittedly, this longer time span allows for greater interference; there is a greater possibility that other, irrelevant stimuli may influence us.

This factor, probably more than any other, contributes to the so-called softness of social-psychological and sociological data. It is very difficult to isolate one's response to anything if, during the response time period, one is also exposed to other stimuli. In the social sciences where the normal time periods are longer than in the physical sciences, this is a major problem. If there is a qualitative difference between the social and physical sciences it rests ultimately with this difference.

The possibility of irrelevant stimuli, however, is a problem that must be dealt with even when dealing with sensory dimensions, as anyone who has attempted to determine the temperature of water with very cold hands can verify.

The fact that we are tempted to treat the intentional dimensions as subjective is due more to our familiarity with the sensory dimensions than to anything inherently subjective about the intentional dimensions. It is only because we have learned to think of the real world as the world defined in terms of these sensory dimensions, that we tend to think of the world defined in any other way as somehow not real.

[27] The term utility is used here and throughout the text to refer to potential use, not in any way to potential for happiness. In effect, what is being argued in the text is that our conception of labour and economic value rests upon our ability to see the causal connection between distinct acts.

[28] Mead (*op. cit.*) clearly sees the connection between our view of the world as possessing its own order and independence and our use of our hands. See pp. 184–185, 248–249, and 362–363. Freud, in contrast, tended to emphasize the genitals in developing his concept of instrumental rationality. Erikson, however, clearly shows that there is a modal affinity between the use of hands and concern with one's genitals in that in both cases there is an intrusive, instrumental orientation. This affinity is reflected in many slang expressions where sexual acts and parts are referred to in labour

terms and where acts of physical labour are referred to in sexual
terms. We talk about 'making' someone or 'making out'. The penis
is referred to as a 'tool'. On the job, on the other hand, it is quite
common to hear someone plead for something or other to 'come'
as he works on it. Adam Smith, Karl Marx, and most classical
economists of course explicitly equated economic value with labour.

[29] Robert MacIver, *Social Causation* (New York: Harper, 1964),
pp. 8ff.

[30] The nature and character of causal relationships has concerned
philosophers and social theorists for centuries; so much has been
written on the subject, in fact, that it is impossible to present a
simple consensus view. Artistotle in his *Physics*, Bk. II, Ch. 3,
presents four types of causes where each type serves to answer the
question 'why?' His four types were material cause, form, efficient
cause and final cause. Only the latter two types of causes, however,
have generally been treated as causes. What they share in common
is the fact that they explain what is to be explained by placing it
within a chain of events. This is the general sense in which the term
'cause' is used in the text and the sense in which, I feel, the term is
best used. Webster's cause, i.e. that which brings about an effect, is
consequently only one type of cause. I might just add that the more
general notion of a causal explanation as one that places an event
within an ordered chain of events is also amenable to dialectical
view of causal change.

[31] Mead, *op. cit.*, pp. 151–164, 252–260.

[32] That social groups generate meanings, values and beliefs
which pertain to the group rather than to the group members can be
called the key sociological insight. For two classical formulations
of the issue, see Durkheim's *Division of Labor in Society*, pp.
39–48, 396ff., and Georg Simmel's essay on Dyads and Triads in
The Sociology of Georg Simmel, pp. 122–142.

[33] For commentaries on man's inclination to order, see Piaget,
and Erikson (bibliography). See also Kurt Goldstein, *The
Organism* (New York: Macmillan & Co., 1939).

[34] For what is perhaps the present day classic sociological for-
mulation of this proposition, see *The Social Construction of
Reality* by Peter Berger and Thomas Luckmann (New York:
Anchor, 1967).

[35] See references in notes 11 and 33.

[36] That prestige is based upon one's ability to order was implicitly recognized by Weber in his analysis of status. This issue will
be dealt with in more detail in Part II.

[37] For a range of interesting articles dealing with this issue, see

Mary Douglas, ed., *Rules and Meanings* (Baltimore: Penguin, 1973).

[38] Some sociologists might object to my use of the terms 'group' and 'groupings'. I use the term as a generic term to refer to any set of individuals who can be thought of as constituting a unified entity. Some sociologists restrict their use of the term to such entities which reflect some sort of internal structure. To have restricted my use of the term in this way would have forced me to use a term such as 'collectivities' which, I fear, would have caused more confusion.

[39] This point has been made in various ways by others. It is central to Weber's concept of *verstehen*. It is a key principle in the sociology of knowledge (see Berger and Luckmann, *The Social Construction of Reality*, New York: Anchor, 1967). It is the central principle of Ethnomethodology (see Garfinkel, Harold, *Studies in Ethnomethodology*, Englewood Cliffs, N.J.: Prentice-Hall, 1967, pp. 1–34). The writings of Alfred Schutz, however, perhaps most bear on this subject (Alfred Schutz, *Collected Papers*, The Hague: Nijhoff, 1962) though his treatment is fundamentally different from that of this essay.

It is also central to Winch, and Louch. For two excellent reviews of this issue in sociological thought, see Richard Bernstein's *Reconstruction of Social and Political Theory* (New York: Harcourt Brace Jonovich, 1976) and Anthony Giddens' *New Rules of Sociological Method* (London: Hutchinson, 1976). This point will be discussed in more detail in Part III.

[40] It might be noted that there is a strong correlation between these various senses of order and the various intentional dimensions. A gratification orientation favours categorizing objects in terms of sets with either positive or negative valences. These sets are then normally related in terms of their valences. One tends, for example, to like friends of friends and enemies of enemies and to dislike enemies of friends and friends of enemies. A power orientation, in contrast, tends to rely more heavily upon the ordering principles of greater than and less than; that is, people and things are ordered in terms of their relative power. A utility/economic orientation meanwhile makes extensive use of the 'if-then' concept of order; things are ordered in terms of 'causal' relationships. An ordering orientation tends to utilize what may be called analogous forms. Situations are ordered in terms of recognized and accepted formal arrangements. This issue will be discussed in greater detail in Part III, pp. 80ff.

[41] The concept of 'ideal type' has a fairly lengthy history in

sociology. It is used here and throughout the text in the Weberian sense to refer to the essential logical form of a particular type. It does not refer to any concrete case nor to any sort of statistical average. See Parsons' discussions of Weber's concept of ideal types in his introduction to Weber's *Theory of Social and Economic Organization*, pp. 8ff. See also Don Martindale, 'Sociological Theory and the Ideal Type' in Llewellyn Gross, ed., *Symposium on Sociological Theory*, (New York: Harper and Row, 1959), pp. 57–91.

PART II: CULTURES, CLASSES, SOCIAL SYSTEMS AND MASSES

[1] The central role of patterns of social contact in the emergence of social groups in contrast to social aggregates has been noted by numerous theorists. See, for example, Durkheim, *The Division of Labor in Society*, pp. 398ff; Homan, *The Human Group*, pp. 82ff; Merton, *Social Theory and Social Structure*, pp. 299ff; Berger and Luckmann, *The Social Construction of Social Reality*, Part II; Mead, *op. cit.*

[2] For the classical statement regarding types of unity, see *The Basic Writings of Aristotle*, pp. 834ff. For an analysis of the concept of unity within the social sciences, see C. W. Smith, *Social Units and Collectivities: A Study of the Logic and Implications of Analytical Units within the Social Sciences* (Ann Arbor, University Microfilms, 1966).

[3] See Berger and Luckmann, *op. cit.*

[4] I should stress here that we shall be analysing various general approaches rather than specific concepts, though there is obviously an overlap between these approaches and their similarly labelled concepts.

[5] This basically neo-Kantian position, as noted in the Introductory Preface, governs this study. It is also what connects it most strongly to the works of Claude Levi-Strauss. See his *Structural Anthropology* (New York: Basic Books, 1963), especially pp. 277ff.

[6] In so far as the term 'culture' is used to refer primarily to meaning systems rather than to the people and their products, it is being used in the more limited sociological sense rather than in the more encompassing anthropological sense. See Everett K. Wilson *Sociology* (Homewood, Ill.: Dorsey Press, 1966) ch. 2.

[7] For a brief but excellent discussion of the various uses of the terms 'culture' and 'subculture' see Oscar Lewis, *A Study of Slum*

Culture: Backgrounds for La Vida (New York: Random House, 1968), pp. 4–21.

[8] The fact that cultures can be broken down into distinctive analytical subsystems, i.e., meaning systems pertinent to gratificational/libidinal, power, economic/labour, and ordering/meaning issues, has methodological advantages. Given a specific event to explain, one can generally find more explicit meanings, definitions and rules with which to explain the event than would be the case if one had to deal with the culture as a whole. One is not dependent upon a single set of generalized definitions, meanings and rules with which to explain all types of behaviour; one rather has four distinct sets, each of which is applicable to those events which reflect the appropriate intentional dimension.

American 'individualism', a cultural value, for example, takes a number of specific forms. At the gratification/libidinal level, it is reflected in the notion of romantic love and the view that each individual should have a dominant voice in the selection of his or her mate; at the political level, it is reflected in the concept of one man-one vote democracy; at the economic level, it is reflected in the spirit of capitalistic 'free enterprise', and individual competition; and at the ordering/religious level, it is reflected in that aspect of the Protestant ethic which stresses man's individual soul and his individual relationship to God.

One could argue that the notion of American individualism belongs more to the past than the present. It is presented here primarily for its heuristic value. For a more detailed analysis of this concept, see Erikson's *Childhood and Society*, chapter VIII, 'Reflections on American Identity.'

[9] For theoretical examples of such distinctions see P. Sorokin, *Society, Culture and Personality* (New York: Harper and Bros., 1947).

[10] It should be stressed that I am here using the term 'culture' in the restricted sense in which it has been defined in the text, namely, meaning systems generated by patterns of social contact which are themselves due to spatial-temporal boundaries.

[11] Perhaps the key theorist in this area is Benjamin Nelson, though there are many others, including Edward Tiryakian. For a good introduction to this type of work, see *Sociological Analysis*, vol. 34,2 (1973) and vol. 36,3 (1975).

[12] See, for example, Ely Chinoy's comments in his *Sociological Perspective* (New York: Random House, 1968), pp. 45ff.

[13] Some theorists, I am sure, will object to this statement. One's

culture does tend to distinguish one from persons belonging to other cultural units. I would argue, however, with Durkheim that this is a secondary property of cultures rather than an essential aspect of any culture.

[14] See Durkheim, *The Division of Labor in Society*, pp. 70ff.

[15] See, for example, Erikson's discussion of the *heyoka* and the *witko* in his *Childhood and Society* (New York: Norton Press, 1950).

[16] For an interesting discussion of this problem, see Oscar Lewis, *A Study of Slum Culture: Backgrounds for La Vida* (New York: Random House, 1968), pp. 7ff.

[17] See Harold Hodges, Jr., *Social Stratification* (Cambridge: Schenkman, 1964), pp. 13–16; and Joseph A. Kahl, *The American Class Structure* (New York: Rinehart and Company, Inc., 1957), pp. 8ff.

[18] See note 1, Part II.

[19] Social categories will be analysed in more detail later. See pp. 68–70.

[20] On Marx, see George Lichtheim, *Marxism: An Historical and Critical Study* (London: Routledge and Kegan Paul, 1961); Bendix and Lipset, 'Karl Marx's Theory of Social Class' in their *Class Status and Power: A Reader in Social Stratification* (New York: Glencoe Free Press, 1957).

[21] There is a fair amount of ambiguity in the use of the term 'class', especially in relationship to Weber. On the one hand, the term is used to refer specifically to economic class, while on the other hand it is used as the generic term to refer to socio-economic strata in general. Unless, otherwise stipulated, I use the term in the latter sense with the proviso that there exists a class meaning system. See Hodges, *op. cit.* and Thomas E. Laswell, *Class and Stratum* (Houghton, Mifflin, Boston, 1965). For an excellent more recent discussion of social class as it relates to Marx and Weber, see Giddons (1973).

[22] See Max Weber, *The Theory of Social and Economic Organization*, (New York: Free Press of Glencoe, 1947) and *From Max Weber*, ed. by Gerth and Mills, (Oxford University Press, 1946) pp. 180ff.

[23] *The Theory of Social and Economic Organization*, p. 428.

[24] Although Weber succeeded in spelling out the major dimensions of social class, (wealth, power and status as defined by him are still the major dimensions used in defining social class) he never rigorously developed the means for empirically measuring these dimensions. It is one thing to recognize that social class

depends on wealth, power and status and quite another thing to construct means for determining the wealth, power and status of any given individual. There is also the related problem of trying to determine the relative importance of each dimension. Not surprisingly, post-Weberian sociologists have attempted to do both these things. As part of this effort, they have tended to utilize a number of secondary class characteristics such as occupation, place of residence, years of education, church affiliation, club affiliations, etc., which can be more easily observed. See Melvin M. Tumin's *Readings on Social Stratification* (Englewood Cliffs: Prentice-Hall, 1970). The use of these secondary class characteristics, however, has not solved the problem of weighting; in fact, in so far as these characteristics tend to incoroporate within themselves elements of wealth, power and status, they serve to complicate proper weighting.

Unfortunately there appears to be no way to avoid the dilemma. Whether the methodological advantages (being able to observe and measure more easily) of these secondary class characteristics outweigh their theoretical disadvantages (not being able to distinguish clearly the parts played by wealth, power and status) is an open question. As might be expected, social scientists engaged in empirical research tend to favour the use of secondary class characteristics while those engaged in more theoretical investigations tend to formulate their questions in terms of the primary class characteristics of wealth, power and status.

Not only must one consider what should be measured in dealing with social class, but there is also the question of how. The situation here is in many ways analogous to that just discussed, since it also pits empirical efficiency against theoretical purity. Here the conflict is not between what characteristics, primary or secondary, are to be used but how are they to be grasped. Are the characteristics to be assigned in terms of various directly perceived qualities of the persons in question or are they to be assigned in terms of the way these persons are seen by their significant others? The first approach entails determining such things as a person's income, years of schooling, etc., and then attempting to construct some sort of class system; the second approach entails determining how a person is ranked by his 'peers' in terms of these general characteristics. The first approach in so far as it relies on 'hard' data has the advantage of being apparently more objective; the second approach in so far as it is tuned in to the ways people actually see and rank each other would appear to be theoretically sounder. Each approach has its limitations. With the first, that it will become reduced to a set of mere social categories; with the second, that it will degenerate into a set of conflicting, highly personal prejudices.

While there are sociologists willing to argue the merits of secondary class characteristics versus primary class characteristics and 'objective' data versus 'reputational' data, neither question deals with the theoretical concerns of this study. They both deal rather with the technical task of discovering social classes in concrete situations. These methodological issues can have theoretical implications; the use of secondary class characteristics and complete reliance on hard data, can produce a class system which is not a class system at all but more a set of social categories. On the other hand, theorists who insist on theoretical purity for their constructs often find that their constructs are useless in analysing concrete situations because they cannot be applied in an agreed manner; denied of empirical support or refutation, such accounts may end up as complex tautologies. In neither situation is either the existence of social classes or their explanatory use questioned; the problem rather is the technical problem of determining how to use social classes to order and explain social behaviour.

It would be misleading, however, to imply that there is a general consensus regarding even the theoretical nature and explanatory powers of social class. The more complex truth is that the technical problems of measurement, etc. have themselves raised other theoretical questions. The actual historical process which gave rise to these questions is too complex to deal with adequately here; let it suffice to say that over the years problems arising out of efforts to use social classes in ordering and explaining social behaviour served to bring into question the very utility of the concept itself. More specifically: Do different societies have different class structures? Do all societies have a class structure? How stable is any given class structure? While the question of the basic utility of social class as a theoretical construct is obviously of immense theoretical importance, it is also quite sterile since one's conclusions will normally be determined by one's initial assumptions. In contrast, the same question has proved most fruitful when asked in an empirical context where it has dealt with the issues of class correlates and class mobility, i.e. movement from class to class. Admittedly, sociologists investigating class correlates and social mobility generally do not claim, at least not explicitly, that they are 'testing' the concept of social class, but in effect that is exactly what they are doing. In so far as they are able to show that a wide range of

136 *A Critique of Sociological Reasoning*

significant characteristics are correlated with different classes, they show the concept to be useful; in so far as they show little to be correlated with social class, they show the concept to have dubious value.

[25] It is admittedly often difficult to distinguish simple interest groups from social classes. For example, Arthur Vidich and Joseph Bensman in *Small Town in Mass Society* (Princeton: Princeton University Press, 1958) refer to the 'traditional farmers' as a specific social class within the middle class. In so far as the traditional farmers share a world view based upon economic, political and prestige similarities, it would seem legitimate to treat them as a social class; on the other hand, the 'particularistic' character of the group makes the practice of referring to them as a social class of dubious value. These, however, are questions of definition and convention and need not concrn us; it is sufficient to recognize the problem. More important, given the aims of this study, is the need to distinguish between two types of interest groups, namely, those which are generated by shared interests and those which give rise to shared interests.

Most interest groups are combinations of these two types. There are usually some shared interests which bring the group together and, once together, the group usually generates other shared interests. Groups vary, however, in their dependency upon one or the other of these two processes. A neighbourhood group may be organized around a common interest such as more regular garbage collection, or it may be organized because the people in the neighbourhood think that such an organization would be a good thing to have to press for whatever programmes the neighbourhood feels are in their interests.

If in the first case the group decides to limit itself to the problem of garbage collection, the group is dependent upon a common interest rather than the interest being an outgrowth of the group. In the second case, in contrast, the interests of the group are likely to evolve in the group. While the members of both types of interest groups have certain interests in common, only the latter type of interest group can be said to have 'group interests', interests which belong to the group rather than to its individual members. It is only the latter type of interests group which can be said to be a true sociological entity; the former type, while self-conscious and organized, remains an aggregate of like-minded individuals (see pp. 39–41). Unless otherwise stated, therefore, I will confine my remarks to interest groups of the latter type.

[26] I refer specifically to interest groups generated by similar

social needs rather than interest groups organized around already existing shared interests. That is I am discussing groups which give rise to shared interests rather than aggregates of individuals. The latter type are often not homogeneous in terms of social class.

[27] The view that social resources are unequally distributed touches on what is probably one of the, if not the, central concerns of the social class approach. It is central to the very notion of a social class and governs the thinking of most class theorists.

[28] I am talking about 'real' social classes, not simply social strata.

[29] There is an extensive literature dealing with the concepts of anomie and alienation. Unfortunately, much of this literature serves more to confuse than to clarify because the fundamental distinction being made in the text is ignored: a distinction which is consistent with Durkheim's definition of anomie and Marx's definition of alienation.

[30] For a brief but excellent discussion of this issue see Herbert Marcuse, *Reason and Revolution* (Boston: Beacon, 1960) pp. 273ff.

[31] See Talcott Parsons, *The Social System* (Glencoe, Ill.: The Free Press, 1951), pp. 24ff.; Peter Blau, *Exchange and Power in Social Life* (New York: John Wiley, 1964), pp. 1ff.; Claude Levi-Strauss, *Structural Anthropology* (New York: Basic Books, 1963), pp. 277–345. While these authors differ in many important ways, they are all in the works cited system/network theorists in the sense that the terms are used in the text. Blau's position in his most recent book, *Inequality and Heterogenity* (New York: Glencoe Free Press, 1977) is another issue. See note 38, Part II.

[32] Those readers not familiar with the terms 'social system' and/or 'exchange network' should not be put off by the discussion that follows. The terms are merely two very common sociological expressions used to designate social groups which exhibit the type of interdependency noted above, e.g., a business organization, a family, a baseball team, etc. The term 'social system' is used to refer to such groups when there clearly is such a group and when the goals and needs of the group dominate; the terms 'social network and exchange network' are used when emphasis is placed on the set of relationships between the parts rather than upon the whole. See Blau, (1964).

[33] The concept of 'units of analysis', should not frighten anyone. It means just what it says and no more, namely, the units, or entities, used in analysing the phenomenon under examination.

[34] See, in addition to Parsons' *Social System, The Structure of*

Social Action (New York: The Free Press of Glencoe, 1949), pp. 43–51, 731ff.

[35] For a general discussion with excellent bibliographical references, see Bruce J. Biddle and Edwin J. Thomas, *Role Theory: Concepts and Research* (New York: John Wiley and Sons, 1966). See also Robert Merton, 'The Role Set: Problems in Sociological Theory,' *British Journal of Sociology* 8 (June): 106–120; Robert Merton, 'Sociological Ambivalence,' in E. Tiryakin, *Sociological Theory, Values and Socio-cultural Change* (New York, Glencoe Free Press, 1963); Erving Goffman, *Encounters* (Indianapolis: Bobbs-Merrill, 1961); Goffman, *Presentation of Self in Everyday Life* (Garden City: Anchor, 1959); and Neal Gross *et al.*, *Explorations in Role Analysis: Studies in the School Superintendency Role* (New York: John Wiley and Sons, 1957).

[36] In order to avoid any confusion it should be clearly stated that most social theorists do not refer to gratification/libidinal, power, utility/economic, or ordering/meaning roles. They are more likely to refer to such roles as father, son, doctor, teacher, politician, minister, boss, secretary, etc. It is generally only upon analysis that one is able to categorize these roles in terms of the intentional dimensions. Parsons has tried to do this by analysing roles in terms of the specific orientations associated with them. In his book *The Social System*, he tried to do this by means of his pattern variables which Parsons sees as covering all possible orientations. Because Parsons' pattern variables cut across the various intentional dimensions, it is difficult to see in *The Social System* that he himself conceives of most roles as having their own intentional bias. In his *Theories of Societies*, however, when he discusses 'Modes of Differentiation within Systems', his emphasis upon kinship, political structures, economic specialization, and religion, clearly reveals his general agreement with the points made in the text. For a more detailed presentation of Parsons' views on this subject see also his *Family, Socialization and Interaction Process* (with Robert F. Bales), Free Press, 1955; and *Toward a General Theory of Action*, ed. with Edward A. Shils, (New York: Harper Torchbooks, 1962).

[37] See Nicholas C. Mullins, *Theories and Theory Groups in Contemporary American Sociology* (New York: Harper and Row, 1973) pp. 39ff.

[38] See Blau, *op. cit.* pp. 12ff and Homans, *The Human Group*, pp. 121ff. A very significant 'sociological' school is also concerned with this issue: I refer to 'symbolic interactionists'. I might simply note that while a good deal of attention has been given to George

Herbert Mead, generally considered the father of the symbolic interaction approach in this study, little attention is given to the symbolic interactionist approach itself. The reason is that despite the fact that it is considered a major sociological approach, analytically it is a social-psychological approach in that it is concerned primarily with meanings *per se* i.e. Level II behaviour, and not meaning systems, i.e. Level III behaviour.

In his most recent book, *Inequality and Heterogeneity: A Primitive Theory of Social Structure* (New York: Free Press, 1977), Blau has retreated even further from the basic sociological vision. In this book he attempts to describe the impact of 'social structure' independent of normative orders *per se*. 'I am a structural determinist, who believes that the structures of objective social positions among which people are distributed exert more fundamental influences on social life than do cultural values and norms, including ultimately the prevailing values and norms.' (p. x) While Blau manages to make a number of interesting observations, let me say that I find his theoretical stand to be so much nonsense. The crux of this nonsense is his belief in 'objective social positions', which he perceives as entailing such things as prestige, power, ethnicity, etc.

[39] See *Theories of Societies*, T. Parsons *et al.*, (New York: The Free Press of Glencoe, 1961), vol. 1, pp. 8–9. For Parsons' original discussion of his Pattern Variables, see *The Social System*, pp. 45ff.

[40] For an excellent review of many of the most relevant dimensions, see Robert Merton's *Social Theory and Social Structure* (New York: Free Press, 1968) pp. 335–380.

[41] See Lewis A. Coser, *The Functions of Social Conflict* (New York: The Free Press, 1954). It is worth noting that Coser, who deserves major credit for forcing modern system theorists to treat conflict seriously, used the writings of Simmel, the foremost exchange theorist among classical social theorists, as a springboard for his own book.

[42] Though it has not been presented in any formal way, a sociological trinity of sorts has been used throughout this study. This trinity could be graphically represented as follows:

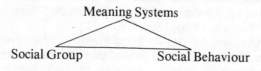

Meaning Systems

Social Group   Social Behaviour

In prose, the sociologist sees social behaviour as governed by meaning systems which belong to social groups. This particular vision would hold equally for all three sociological approaches presented above.

It is possible, nevertheless, to analyse the various sociological approaches in terms of this sociological trinity. More specifically, it is possible to show that each approach tends to have a bias for one particular point of the trinity, and tends to favour or emphasize either meaning systems, social groups or social behaviour. Why this is so, I am not sure; that it is so, however, I am positive. I am furthermore equally sure that each particular affinity reveals certain essential aspects of each approach though I am not sure what comes first, the affinity or the essential aspect.

Simply put, the socio-cultural approach favours meaning systems; the social class approach, social groups; and the social system/social network approach, social behaviour. All of these affinities have already been noted. The socio-cultural approach tends to view both persons and their behaviour in terms of the governing meaning systems; this is perhaps best evidenced by the habit of referring to the people and their behaviour as simply part of the culture. Social class and interest group theorists, in contrast, focus upon the persons who make up the social groups; their primary focus is nearly always the 'warm bodies'; class meaning systems and class behaviour are seen to follow from the social group, i.e. the class. Social system and exchange theorists meanwhile focus their attention upon the social behaviour itself. This was clearly revealed in even our brief analysis of Parsons' theory of social action. Meanings and meaning systems, as well as social groups themselves, are seen to emerge from social behaviour.

For a related but different treatment of this subject see George Ritzer's *Sociology: A Multiple Paradigm Science* (Boston: Allyn and Baco, 1975).

[43] See Gustave Le Bon, *The Crowd* (London: T. F. Unwin, 1921); Sigmund Freud, *Group Psychology and the Analysis of the Ego* (New York: Bantam Books, 1960); Ralph Turner and Lewis M. Killian, *Collective Behavior* (Englewood Cliffs: Prentice-Hall, 1957); and Stanley Milgram and Hans Toch, 'Collective Behavior: Crowds and Social Movements' in *The Handbook of Social Psychology*, ed. Lindzey and Aronson (Reading, Mass.: Addison-Wesley, 1968), vol. IV, pp. 507–610.

[44] See Aristotle, *op. cit.* My use of Aristotle's four types of unity may seem forced. I would argue that it simply indicates the analytical power of Aristotle's original analysis. I might add that the relevancy of Aristotle's analysis, like that of Kant's, is due to

the fact that both Aristotle and Kant were, to use Strawson's expression, 'descriptive metaphysicians'. They were concerned with spelling out the categories of human experience, not with imposing on human experience their own categories. In this regard, both Aristotle and Kant were sociologists as well as philosophers.

[45] On social conformity, see Milgram and Toch, *op. cit.* and S. E. Asch, *Social Psychology* (New York: Prentice-Hall, 1952). Though I referred to Freud's *Group Psychology* in note 43, a word of clarification is required at this point. Though Freud was interested in accounting for the mass-like quality of much group behaviour, his primary concern was not masses *per se*, but rather social groups. For Freud such groups are not mindless; rather they are governed by a shared 'ego ideal'. Nevertheless, even with Freud, groups characterized by 'panic' become mindless.

[46] For an excellent analysis of this process, see Georg Simmel, 'On the Significance of Numbers for Social Life', in *The Sociology of Georg Simmel*, ed. and trans. by Kurt Wolff (New York: The Free Press, 1964).

[47] See Purcell, in Daniel Lerner, *Parts and Wholes* (New York: The Free Press of Glencoe, 1963); and H. Blumer, 'Collective Behavior', in Alfred McClung Lee, *Principles of Sociology* (New York: Barnes and Noble, 1955).

[48] There are two distinct types of hybrids which should not be confused: analytic hybrids and 'concrete' hybrids. Concrete hybrids cannot be avoided; most concrete social groups have elements of more than one ideal type. When dealing with analytical types, however, it is generally advisable not to deal with hybrids unless one has clearly stipulated that one has done so. We will discuss this issue in more detail shortly.

[49] R. W. Brown, 'Mass Phenomena', in *The Handbook of Social Psychology* (Cambridge, Mass.: Addison-Wesley, 1954), vol. II, pp. 833–876.

[50] Milgram and Toch, *op. cit.*, pp. 550ff.

[51] For an excellent discussion of this issue, see Aaron Circourel, *Method and Measurement in Sociology* (New York: The Free Press, 1964), chapter V, 'The Demographic Method'.

[52] Talcott Parsons, *The Social System*, pp. 326ff.

[53] Parsons is himself perfectly aware of these facts.

[54] See Claude Levi-Strauss, *op. cit.*, especially his references to A. R. Ratcliffe-Brown.

[55] See pp. 46ff.

PART III: THE SOCIOLOGICAL VISION OF MEANING

[1] This in my opinion is probably the basic insight of sociology though unfortunately many contemporary sociologists refuse to recognize it. I might add that it is a view which has been shared by various philosophers, including most pragmatists and Wittgenstein. Fortunately, it is an issue which recently has begun to generate more concern. Here I would strongly recommend two books which deal with this issue in a different though parallel way: Habermas's *Legitimation Crisis, ob. cit.* and Giddens' *New Rules of Sociological Method, ob. cit.*

[2] See Emil Durkheim's *Division of Labour in Society, op. cit.*, pp. 396ff.

[3] See his *Structural Anthrolopology, op. cit.*, Ch. XV and XVI.

[4] In this regard, I might just suggest what I feel would be a potentially very productive line of investigation, namely, an attempt to analyse meaning systems in terms of different types of logical/mathematical systems. My use of the concepts of 'sets'—'greater than and less than', 'if-then'—represents one of the directions in which, I feel, such an analysis might go.

[5] W. F. Whyte, *Street Corner Society* (Chicago: University of Chicago Press, 1955). See especially pp. 104–255.

[6] *Ibid.*, p. 230.

[7] S. A. Stouffer *et al.*, *The American Soldier* (New York: John Wiley and Sons, 1965).

[8] *Ibid.*, p. 107.

[9] *Ibid.*, pp. 112–130.

[10] *Ibid.*, pp. 112–146.

[11] *Ibid.*, pp. 364–370.

[12] Bruno Bettelheim, *The Informed Heart* (New York: The Free Press of Glencoe, 1960).

[13] *Ibid.*, pp. 171–172.

[14] For a more sociological sensitive study of the German concentration camp, see Paul Neurath, *Social Life in the German Concentration Camps Dachau and Buchenwald* (Ann Arbor: University Microfilms, 1951).

[15] Bettelheim, *op. cit.*, pp. 161–166.

[16] See Neurath, *op. cit.*

[17] *Ibid.*, p. 204.

[18] *Ibid.*, pp. 219–220.

[19] *Ibid.*, pp. 209–212.

[20] For what I consider to be one of the most sociologically sophisticated treatments of persons living under 'concentration

camp' conditions see the *Shantung Compound*, by Langdon Gilkey (New York: Harper Row, 1966). Although Gilkey is not a sociologist, his analysis is extremely sensitive to the sociological issues raised in this study.

[21] C. Wright Mills, *White Collar* (New York: The Oxford University Press, 1956).

[22] In this discussion both the power and economic dimensions are used in the manner in which they have previously been defined, i.e. as analytically distinct. Some 'Marxists' may claim that this is not the case, especially not with Mills. This is one of those issues which can be argued indefinitely without any resolution. I find as much, if not more, Weber in Mills as Marx and believe that Mills saw political and economic resources as analytically distinct if factually interrelated.

[23] *Ibid.*, p. 39.

[24] *Ibid.*, pp. 342–343.

[25] Max Weber, *The Protestant Ethic and the Spirit of Capitalism* (New York: Charles Scribner's Sons, 1958).

[26] Few modern Marxists would take this view; with some justification, they could claim that no 'good' Marxist ever did. It was, however, the dominant view of what the Marxist view was when Weber wrote the *Protestant Ethic*.

[27] See especially the articles by Pope, Cohen, and Hazelrigg: 'De-Parsonizing Weber: A Critique of Parsons' Interpretation of Weber's Sociology', *American Sociological Review* (April, 1975), vol. 40, no. 2; 'On the Divergence of Weber and Durkheim: A Critique of Parsons' Convergence Thesis', *American Sociological Review* (August, 1975), vol. 40, no. 4; and 'Classic on Classic: Parsons' Interpretation of Durkheim', *American Sociological Review* (August, 1973), vol. 38, no. 4.

[28] It might just be noted here that even in his analysis of bureaucratic structures, Weber emphasizes the self-interest character of bureaucrats rather than their, more commonly noted, integrative concerns.

[29] Emil Durkheim, *The Division of Labor in Society* (New York: The Free Press of Glencoe, 1964), p. 278.

[30] Max Weber, *The Theory of Social and Economic Organization* (New York: The Free Press of Glencoe, 1947), p. 115.

[31] It is very difficult to document this assertion since most 'ethnomethdologists' don't claim to be ethnomethodologists; furthermore, they generally refrain from defining themselves and their point of view in these general terms. I can only assert that, based upon my own conversations with persons considered by

others to be ethnomethdologists, the statement is true.

[32] I am not sure, but I believe that Giddens suggested a similar approach when he wrote '...rather than, in some sense, the concepts of sociology having to be open to rendition in terms of lay concepts, it is the case that the observing social scientist has to be able first to grasp those lay concepts, i.e., penetrate hermeneutically the form of life whose features he wishes to analyse or explain.' In addition, I should note that there are some sociologists who are engaged in exactly this type of work though their approach differs somewhat from my own. I refer here specifically to Edward Tiryakian and Benjamin Nelson. See especially Tiryakian's article 'Neither Marx nor Durkheim...Perhaps Weber', *American Journal of Sociology* (July, 1975), vol. 81, no. 1; and Nelson's 'Civilizational Complexes and Intercivilizational Encounters', *Sociological Analysis*, 1973, vol. 34, no. 2.

Some readers may feel that I am here, and elsewhere, unfairly ignoring the work of those most directly engaged in this type of research, namely the sociologists of sociology. While there is definitely an affinity between the works of these persons (see especially Robert W. Friedrich, *A Sociology of Sociology*, New York, Free Press, 1970 and Reynolds and Reynolds, eds., and *The Sociology of Sociology*, New York: David McKay, 1970), there is a crucial difference which explains why I have deliberately avoided examining these works in this study. The sociologists of sociology are primarily interested in examining the social roots and social impact of different sociological theories rather than analysing the underlying cognitive structures of such theories. As a result their main concern is with what I would call the concrete 'accidental' or 'secondary' characteristics of such theories whereas mine is with their essential cognitive forms. Any attempt to deal with both types of characteristics at the same time, I have found, serves only to foster confusion since the foci of concern are quite different.

A sociology of sociology which utilizes the central concepts of this study is possible, but it would be quite different in form from that of Friedrich's. More specifically it would look at sociology in terms of the major sociological approaches described above, i.e., as a cultural phenomenon, a reflection of class ideology, and as a product of the division of labour. I have briefly sketched out what the form of such a sociology of sociology would be in my concluding comments.

[33] Simmel, *op. cit.* p. 23.

PART IV SUMMARY AND CONCLUDING COMMENTS

¹ Russell Dynes, 'Sociology as a Religious Movement,' *The American Sociologist*, vol. 9, No. 4, 1974, pp. 169–176.
² See Karl Mannheim's, *Ideology and Utopia* (New York: Harvest Book, 1936), especially chapters II and III.
³ Not surprisingly, Parsons seems to hold this view. This is most clearly shown by his continual reference to personality, social and cultural systems as constituting the respective fields of psychologists, sociologists, and anthropologists.
⁴ See for example Mullins, *op. cit.*
⁵ Personal communication, 1963.
⁶ Simmel, *op. cit.*, p. 23.

Bibliography

Adler, Alfred. *The Individual Psychology of Alfred Adler*, edited and annotated by Henry L. & Rowene R. Ansbacher (New York: Basic Books, 1956)

Aristotle, *The Basic Works of Aristotle*, ed by Richard McKoon (New York: Random House, 1941)

Asch, S. E. *Social Psychology* (New York: Prentice-Hall, 1952)

Bendix Reinhart and Lipset, Seymour Martin (*Class Status and Power: A Reader in Social Stratification* (Glencoe: The Free Press, 1957)

Berger, Peter and Luckmann, Thomas. *The Social Construction of Reality*, (New York: Anchor Book, 1967)

Bergson, Henri. *Creative Evolution* (New York: Modern Library, 1944)

Bernstein, Richard. *Reconstruction of Social and Political Theory* (New York: Harcourt Brace Jovanovich, 1976)

Bettelheim, Bruno. *The Informed Heart* (New York: The Free Press of Glencoe, 1960)

Biddle, Bruce and Thomas, Edwin. *Role Theory: Concepts and Research* (New York: John Wiley and Sons, 1966)

Blau, Peter. *Exchange and Power in Social Life* (New York: John Wiley, 1964) *Inequality and Heterogeneity* (New York: Free Press, 1977)

Blumer, H. 'Collective Behavior,' in Lee, Alfred McClung, *Principles of Sociology* (New York: Barnes and Noble, 1955)

Brown, R. W. 'Mass Phenomena' in *The Handbook of Social Psychology* (Cambridge, Mass.: Addison-Wesley, 1954)

Chinoys, Ely. *Sociological Perspective* (New York: Random House, 1968)

Circourel, Aaron. *Method and Measurement in Sociology* (New York: The Free Press, 1964)

Coser, Lewis A. *The Functions of Social Conflict* (New York: The Free Press, 1954)

Dewey, John. *Experience and Nature* (New York: Macmillan, 1929)

Douglas, Mary ed. *Rules and Meanings* (Baltimore: Penguin, 1973)

Durkheim, Emile. *The Division of Labor in Society* (New York: Free Press, 1956) *The Elementary Forms of Religious Life* (New York: Free Press, 1954)

Dynes, Rusell, 'Sociology as a Religious Movement,' *The American Sociologist*, vol. 9, No. 4, 1974

Erikson, Erik. *Childhood and Society* (New York: Norton, 1950)

Friedrich, Robert W. *A Sociology of Sociology* (New York: Free Press, 1970)

Freud, Sigmund. *Group Psychology and the Analysis of the Ego* (New York: Bantam Books, 1960)

Garfinkel, Harold. *Studies in Ethnomethodology* (Engelwood Cliffs, N. J.: Prentice-Hall, 1967)

Gerth, H. H. and Mills, C. Wricht, ed. *From Max Weber* (Oxford University Press, 1946)

Giddens, Anthony. *The Class Structure of the Advanced Societies* (London: Hutchinson & Co., 1973). *New Rules of Sociological Method* (London: Hutchinson & Co., 1976)

Gilkey, Langdon. *Shantung Compound* (New York: Harper Row, 1966)

Goffman, Erving. *Encounters* (Indianapolis: Bobbs Merill, 1961) *Presentation of Self in Everyday Life* (Garden City: Anchor, 1959)

Goldstein, Kurt. *The Organism* (New York: Macmillan, 1939)

Gross, Neal et al., *Explorations in Role Analysis: Studies in the School Superintendency Role* (New York: John Wiley & Sons, 1951)

Habermas, Jurgen, *The Legitimation Crisis* (Boston: Beacon Press, 1975)

Hampshire, Stuart. *Thought and Action* (London: Chatto and Winclus, 1959)

Harré, R. and Secord, P. F. *The Explanation of Social Behavior* (Oxford: Basil Blackwell, 1972)

Hodges, Harold Jr., *Social Stratification* (Cambridge: Schenkman, 1964)

Homans, George. *The Human Group* (New York: Harcourt, Brace, 1950)

Hume, David. *Enquiries Concerning the Human Understanding and Concerning the Principles of Morals*, (Oxford: The Clarendon Press, 1966).

Kahl, Joseph A. *The American Class Structure* (N.Y.: Rinehart and Co., 1957)

Kant, Immanuel, *Critique of Pure Reason* (London: Macmillan & Co., 1958)

Kuhn, Thomas. *The Structure of Scientific Reasoning* (Chicago: Chicago University Press, 1962/1970)

Lamprecht, Sterling P. *Our Philosophical Tradition* New York: Appelton-Century Croft, 1955)

Lasswell, Thomas E. *Class and Stratum* (Boston: Houghton & Mifflin, 1965)

Le Bon, *The Crowd* (London: T. F. Unwin, 1921)

Lenski, Gehard E. *Power and Privilege* (New York: McGraw Hill, 1966)

Lerner, Daniel. *Parts and Wholes* (New York: The Free Press of Glencoe, 1963)

Levi-Strauss, Claude. *Structural Anthropology* (N.Y.: Basic Books, 1963)

Lewis, C. I. *Mind and the World Order* (New York: Dover, 1956)

Lewis, Oscar. *A Study of Slum Culture: Backgrounds for La Vida* (New York: Random House, 1968)

Lichtheim, George. *Marxism: An Historical and Critical Study* (London: Routledge and Kegan Paul, 1961)

Lorenz, Konrad. *On Agression* (New York: Harcourt, Brace & World, 1966)

Louch, A. R. *Explanation and Human Action* (Berkeley, Calif.: University of California Press, 1969)

Manheim, Karl. *Ideology and Utopia* (New York: Harvest Book, 1936)

Marcuse, Herbert. *Reason and Revolution* (New York: Oxford University Press, 1941)

Martindale, Don. 'Sociological Theory and the Ideal Type' in *Symposium on Sociological Theory* ed. Llewellyn Gross (N.Y.: Harper and Row, 1959)

Merton, Robert 'The Role Set: Problems in Sociological Theory,' *British Journal of Sociology* 8 (June): 106–120. Social Theory and Social Structure (Glencoe: Free Press, 1957). 'Sociological Ambivalence,' in E. Tiryakian, *Sociological Theory, Values and Socio-cultural Change* (New York: Free Press, 1963)

Milgram, Stanley and Toch, Hans 'Collective Behavior: Crowds and Social Movements' in *The Handbook of Social Psychology* ed. Lindzey and Aronson (Reading, Mass.: Addison-Wesley, 1968) vol. IV pp. 507–610

Mills, Wright. *White Collar* (New York: The Oxford University Press, 1956)

Morris, Desmond. *The Naked Ape* (New York: McGraw Hill, 1962)

Mullins, Nicholas C. *Theories and Theory Groups in Contemporary American Sociology* (New York: Harper and Row, 1973)

Nelson, Benjamin 'Civilization Complexes and Inter-civilizational Encounters,' *Sociological Analysis*. 1973 vol. 34 No. 2

Neurath, Paul. *Social Life in the German Concentration Camps Dachau and Buchenwald* (Ann Arbor: University Microfilms, 1951)

Parson, Talcott and Bales, Robert. *Family, Socialization and Interaction Process* (New York: Free Press of Glencoe, 1955); *The Social System* (Glencoe: Free Press, 1951); *The Structure of Social Action* (Glencoe: Free Press, 1949); et al *Theories of Societies* (New York: Free Press of Glencoe, 1961); *Toward a General Theory of Action* (ed. with Edward Shils) (New York: Harper Torchbooks, 1962)

Peirce, Charles Sanders. The Philosophy of Peirce: *Selected Writings*, ed. Justus Buchler (London: Kegan Paul, 1940)

Piaget, Jean. *Judgment and Reasoning in the Child* (Paterson, N. J.: Littlefield, Adam & Co., 1959); *The Child's Conception of the World* (Paterson, N. J.: Littlefield, Adam & Co., 1960); *Psychology of Intelligence* (Paterson, N.J.: Littlefield, Adam & Co., 1960); *The Moral Judgment of the Child* (New York: Collins Books, 1962); *The Origins of Intelligence of the Child* (New York: Norton, 1963)

Pope, Whitney, Cohen Jere, and Hazellrigg, Lawrence. 'De Parsonizing Weber: A Critique of Parsons' Interpretation of Weber's Sociology,' *American Sociological Review* (August, 1975) vol. 40 no. 2; 'On the Divergence of Weber and Durkheim: A critique of Parsons' Convergence Thesis,' *American Sociological Review* (August, 1975) vol. 40 No. 4; 'Classic on Classic: Parsons' Interpretation of Durkheim,' *American Sociological Review* (August, 1973) vol. 38 No. 4

Quine, Willard Van Ormon, *Word and Object* (New York: Wiley, 1960)

Reynolds and Reynolds ed. *The Sociology of Sociology* (New York: David McKay, 1970)
Riesman, David, with Glazer Nathan and R. Denney. *The Lonely Crowd* (Garden City: Doubleday Anchor Books, 1953)
Ritzer, George. *Sociology: A Multiple Paradigm Science* (Boston: Allyn and Bacon, 1975)

Scheffler, Israel. *Science and Subjectivity* (Indianapolis, New York, Kansas City: Bobbs Merrill, 1967)
Schutz, Alfred. *Collected Papers* ed. by Maurice Natanson (The Hague: Nijhoff 1962)
Simmel, George. *The Sociology of George Simmel* ed. and trans. by Kurt Wolff (New York: The Free Press, 1964)
Smith, C. W. *Social Units and Collectivities: A Study of the Logic and Implications of Analytical Units Within The Social Sciences* (Ann Arbor, University Microfilms, 1966)
Sorokin, P. *Society, Culture and Personality* (New York: Harper and Bros., 1947)
Stouffer, S. A., et al. *The American Soldier* (New York: John Wiley and Sons, 1965)
Strawson, P. *Individuals* (London: Methuen, 1959)
Sullivan, Harry Stack. *The Interpersonal Theory of Psychiatry* (New York: Norton Co., 1953)

Tiryakian, E. 'Neither Marx nor Durkheim . . . Perhaps Weber,' *American Journal of Sociology* (July, 1975) vol. 81 No. 1 *Sociological Theory Values and Socio-Cultural Change* (New York: Free Press, 1963)
Turner, Ralph and Killian, Lewis. *Collective Behavior* (Englewood Cliffs: Prentice-Hall, 1957)

Weber, Max. *The Protestant Ethic and the Spirit of Capitalism* (New York: Charles Scribner's Sons, 1958); *The Theory of Social and Economic Organization* (New York: Free Press of Glencoe, 1947)

Wilson, Edward O. *Sociobiology: The New Synthesis* (Cambridge, Belknap Press, 1975)

Wilson, Everett K. *Sociology* (Homewood, Ill.: Dorsey, 1966)

Whitehead, Alfred North. *Process and Reality* (New York: Macmillan, 1929); *Science and the Modern World* (New York: Macmillan, 1925)

Whyte, W. F. *Street Corner Society* (Chicago: University of Chicago Press, 1955)

Winch, Peter. *The Idea of a Social Science* (London: Routledge and Kegan Paul, 1958)

Wittgenstein, Ludwig. *Philosophical Investigations* (New York: Macmillan, 1953)

Index

Adler, Alfred, 123n
Alienation, 47ff
Anomie, 47ff
Anthropology, 28, 131n
Ardrey, Robert, 28
Aristotle, 129n, 140n
Aron, R., 115
Aronson, Elliot, 123n, 141n
Asch, Solomon, 141n

Bales, Robert, 138n
Behaviourism, 9, 28, 123nff
Bendix, R., 133n
Bensman, Joseph, 136n
Berger, Peter, 129n, 130n, 131n
Berger, Seymour, 123n
Bergson, Henri, 8, 123n
Bernstein, Richard, ii, 121n, 127n
Bettelheim, Bruno, 90, 94ff, 142n
Biddle, Bruce, 138n
Blau, Peter, 57–58, 137n, 138n, 139n
Blumer, H., 141n
Brown, R. W., 65, 141n

Categories of experience, 1, 3
Causality, 3, 16ff
Chinoy, Ely, 132n
Cicourel, Aaron, 141n
Cohen, Jere, 143n
Comte, A., 115
Coser, Lewis, 139n
Crowds, 64ff
Culture, 32ff, 39ff, 131n, 139nff

Demography, 70
Dewey, John, ii, 8
Douglas, Mary, 130n
Durkheim, Emile, 39, 79, 102ff, 115, 129n, 133n, 142n, 143n
Dynes, Russel, 115, 145n

Economics, 28, 83ff
Erikson, Erik, 122n, 128n, 129n, 132n, 133n
Ethnomethodology, 87, 108ff, 130n, 143n

Flavell, John, 122n
Freud, Sigmund, 80, 81, 128n, 140n, 141n
Friedrich, Robert, 144n

Garfinkel, Harold, 130n
Gerth, Hans, 133n
Giddens, Anthony, ii, 2, 130n, 142n, 144n
Gilkey, Langdon, 142n
Goffman, Erving, 138n
Goldstein, Kurt, 129n
Gross, Llewellyn, 131n
Gross, Neal, 138n

Habermas, Jurgens, ii, 2, 142n
Hampshire, Stuart, 122n, 123n
Hazelrigg, Lawrence, 143n
Hodges, Harold, 133n
Homans, George, 57, 131n, 138n
Hughes, E., 117
Hume, David, 121n